Places In Time
A Kid's Historic Guide to the Changing Names and Places of the World

A Brief Political and Geographic History of

Europe

Where Are . . . Prussia, Gaul, and the Holy Roman Empire

Mitchell Lane PUBLISHERS

P.O. Box 196
Hockessin, Delaware 19707
Visit us on the web: www.mitchelllane.com
Comments? email us: mitchelllane@mitchelllane.com

Places In Time
A Kid's Historic Guide to the Changing Names and Places of the World

Titles in the Series

A Brief Political and Geographic History of . . .

Africa
Where Are Belgian Congo, Rhodesia, and Kush?

Asia
Where Are Saigon, Kampuchea, and Burma?

Europe
Where Are Prussia, Gaul, and the Holy Roman Empire?

Latin America
Where Are Gran Colombia, La Plata, and Dutch Guiana?

The Middle East
Where Are Persia, Babylon, and the Ottoman Empire?

North America
Where Are New France, New Netherland, and New Sweden?

Places In Time
A Kid's Historic Guide to the Changing Names and Places of the World

A Brief Political and
Geographic History of

Europe

Where Are... Prussia, Gaul, and the Holy Roman Empire

Frances E. Davey

Mitchell Lane
PUBLISHERS

P.O. Box 196
Hockessin, Delaware 19707
Visit us on the web: www.mitchelllane.com
Comments? email us: mitchelllane@mitchelllane.com

Printing   1   2   3   4   5   6   7   8   9

Library of Congress Cataloging-in-Publication Data
Davey, Frances E.
   A brief political and geographic history of Europe : where are Prussia, Gaul, and the Holy Roman Empire? / by Frances E. Davey.
      p. cm. — (Places in time—a kid's historic guide to the changing names and places in the world)
   Includes bibliographical references and index.
   ISBN-13: 978-1-58415-625-3 (lib. bnd.)
   1. Europe—History—Juvenile literature. 2. Europe—Historical geography—Juvenile literature. I. Title.
D102.D25 2007
940—dc22

                                                                        2007000796

PHOTO CREDITS: Maps by Jonathan Scott—pp. 6, 7, 8, 16, 21, 24, 32, 40, 48, 56, 64, 72, 80, 88; p. 10—Museum of London/Heritage Images; pp. 11, 26, 27, 28, 30, 37, 46 (right), 47, 50, 52, 53, 61, 66, 67, 82, 83—JupiterImages; pp. 12, 18, 31, 55, 59, 60, 68, 74, 78, 84, 86, 93—Wikimedia Commons; p. 13—Guildhall Art Gallery; p. 14—Library of Congress; p. 19—Lionel-Noel Royer; p. 20—Vincenzo Camuccini; p. 22—Crew Creative; p. 23—Roy Miles Gallery, London; p. 29—Jules Eugène Lenepveu; p. 34—Martii Mustonen; p. 35—Galleria degli Uffizi; p. 36—Uffizi, Florence; p. 38—Rijksmuseum, Amsterdam; p. 43—Pierre Lenfant; p. 44—(left) Anton Graff, (right) Martin van Meytens; p. 45—Alexander Kotzebue; p. 46 (left)—Allan Ramsey/Scottish National Portrait Gallery; p. 51—Duplessis; p. 54—Robinson; p. 58—Jean-Baptiste Isabey; p. 62—Augustus Pugin and Thomas Rowlandson; p. 69—Georg Bleibtreu; p. 70—Franz Xavier Winterhalter; p. 76—maps by Andrea Pickens; p. 85—Naval Historical Center; p. 87—Robert Hunt Library; p. 90—NASA; p. 91—European Union/European Commission; p. 92—Sharon Beck; p. 94—European Commission; p. 95—Senate of Berlin.

PUBLISHER'S NOTE: This story is based on the author's extensive research, which she believes to be accurate. Documentation of such research is contained on page 104.

The internet sites referenced herein were active as of the publication date. Due to the fleeting nature of some web sites, we cannot guarantee they will all be active when you are reading this book.

To reflect current usage, we have chosen to use the secular era designations BCE ("before the common era") and CE ("of the common era") instead of the traditional designations BC ("before Christ") and AD (*anno Domini,* "in the year of the Lord").

                                                                        PLB

Places In Time

Table of Contents

Map of Europe...6
Introduction 7
Chapter 1   The Great Fire of London 9
Chapter 2   The Rise and Fall of Rome.......................17
For Your Information: Cleopatra, Queen of Egypt...................23
Chapter 3   The Middle Ages................................25
For Your Information: The Black Death.............................31
Chapter 4   The Golden Age.................................33
For Your Information: The Holy Roman Empire 39
Chapter 5   The Old Regime Turns New 41
For Your Information: The Scientific Revolution 47
Chapter 6   A Time of Revolution...........................49
For Your Information: "Let Them Eat Cake" 55
Chapter 7   A Century of Isms..............................57
For Your Information: Germany and Gymnastics 63
Chapter 8   The Birth of the Nation-State 65
For Your Information: A Revolution of a Different Kind............71
Chapter 9   Imperialism and the Great War 73
For Your Information: Barbed Wire and Big Berthas 79
Chapter 10   World War II and the Cold War 81
For Your Information: The Holocaust.............................87
Chapter 11   From Iron Curtain to European Union 89
For Your Information: German Reunification......................95
Timeline...96
Chapter Notes 100
Further Reading..104
    Books..104
    Works Consulted 104
    On the Internet...106
Glossary..107
Index 108

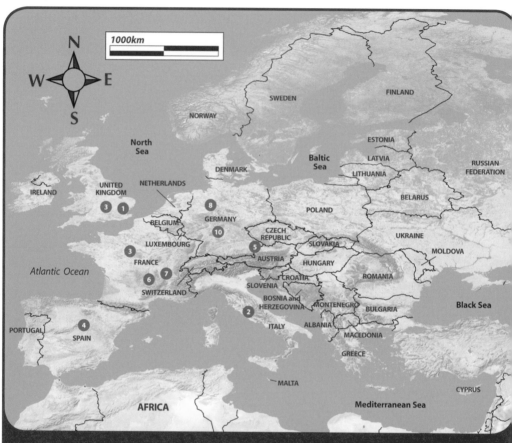

Modern-day Europe. Centuries of political and religious uprisings led to the creation of a modern Europe. While European countries still have disagreements, their borders are fairly stable. Each circled number corresponds to the chapter in which the area is discussed. Chapters 9 and 11 cover events that involved the entire continent.

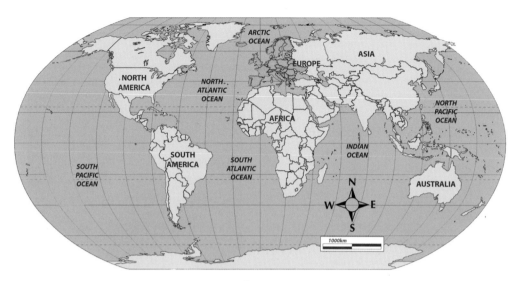

Where Are . . . Prussia, Gaul, and the Holy Roman Empire

Introduction

"The function of the historian is . . . to master and understand [the past] as the key to the understanding of the present." Historian E. H. Carr wrote these words in the mid-twentieth century. However, they apply to any period and any place. In this book, you will examine the role of politics and geography in the history of Western Europe. Western Europe has always been a busy place. Over the last two millennia, kingdoms and countries clashed over religious and political differences while also forming alliances. Royalty and military men achieved immortality by defeating—or being defeated by—their enemies. Droughts and vermin killed untold numbers of people. During periods of turmoil, Western Europeans saw their world change, seemingly overnight. During periods of calm, things seemed to stay the same for generations. But through it all, Western Europe has remained a region of great diversity, and continues to change today.

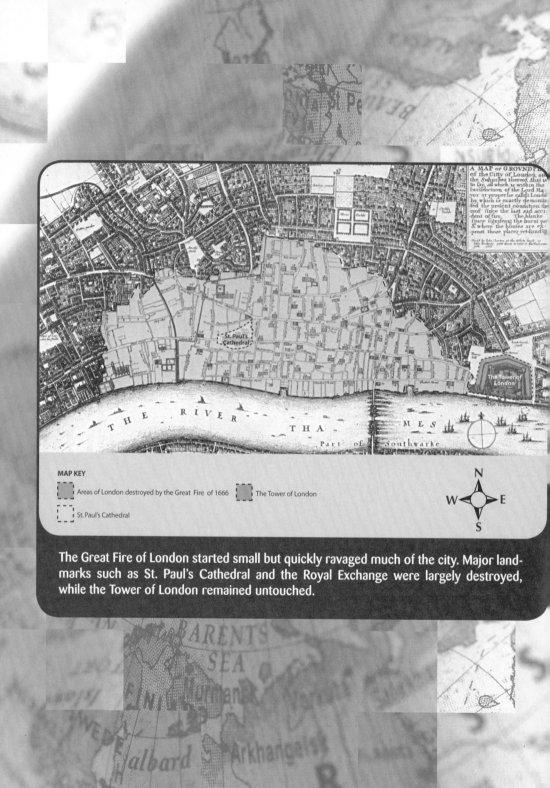

A MAP or GROVND-PLO
of the Citty of London an
the Suburbes thereof that is
to say all which is within the
Iurisdiction of the Lord Mayor or proper lie called London
by which is exactly demonitra-
ted the present condition the
rent since the last sad accident of fire. The blanke
space signifying the burnt par
& where the houses are ex-
prest those places yet standing

St. Paul's
Cathedral

The Tower of
London

THE . RIVER . . THA . . . MES

Part of Southwarke

MAP KEY

Areas of London destroyed by the Great Fire of 1666   The Tower of London

St. Paul's Cathedral

N
W E
S

The Great Fire of London started small but quickly ravaged much of the city. Major land-marks such as St. Paul's Cathedral and the Royal Exchange were largely destroyed, while the Tower of London remained untouched.

The Great Fire of London

The summer of 1666 in London had been long, hot, and dry. Like everyone else, Thomas Farriner, a baker, wanted the heat to end. His bakery shop occupied the ground floor of his house in Pudding Lane. On the night of September 1, he carefully checked the six fireplaces he used to bake bread to make sure the fires had been extinguished. Then he went upstairs to bed.

He hadn't checked his fireplaces carefully enough. Shortly after midnight, the smell of smoke and the crackling of flames woke him up. His house was on fire! As the flames licked upward, Farriner, his daughter, and a servant scrambled out a window and onto the steep roof of their neighbor's house. Farriner's maidservant, however, was too frightened. She stayed inside the house and perished in the fire.[1]

Farriner and his neighbors threw buckets of water on the inferno, their eyes watering from the smoke and their lungs straining for air. The fire continued to burn. Finally, the parish constables arrived and ordered the neighboring houses to be torn down to keep the fire from spreading. When Farriner's neighbors protested, Sir Thomas Bloodworth, the lord mayor of London, backed them up. He didn't realize how serious the fire was. "A woman might piss it out,"[2] he said.

Bloodworth had made a fatal decision. By seven o'clock that morning—Sunday, September 2, 1666—the fire was out of control. Pushed by an easterly gale, it roared toward the River Thames and consumed everything in its path. Hundreds of houses, riverfront warehouses, and structures lining London Bridge burned to the ground. Men, women, and children rushed to save their furniture, clothing, and other belongings. Those who could afford

The original St. Paul's Cathedral was destroyed in the Great Fire of London. Londoners scrambled to flee the area, carrying their belongings through jam-packed streets.

it hastily hired boats to row their families and goods across the river to safety.

King Charles II finally ordered buildings near the fire to be demolished, but he was too late. As the day wore on, Londoners stopped trying to put out the flames and just fled. Thousands clogged the narrow streets, pushing carts, carrying blankets filled with their possessions, pulling small children away from danger. Many stopped to pray at small churches that had not yet been touched by flames; others kept moving. Firefighters found it nearly impossible to worm their way through the crowds to the fire—not that their efforts would have made much of a difference. Many simply gave up and joined the mass exodus.

First Anglo-Dutch War begins

1087   1654

1652

Construction starts on
St. Paul's Cathedral

First Anglo-Dutch War ends

The Great Fire of London

As Monday, September 3 dawned, the fire rushed toward London's commercial center. The Royal Exchange, home to numerous fancy shops, provided fodder for the flames. The city's wealthier residents, who at first did not believe the fire would ever reach them, began to fear they would lose their worldly goods. In desperation, they paid poor Londoners exorbitant amounts of money to pile their belongings in carts and move them away from the fire. Not surprisingly, thievery was rampant. By that evening, the Thames was clogged with barges and smaller boats as shopkeepers tried to save their wares and householders scrambled to salvage their belongings.

John Evelyn, a wealthy London resident, watched in horror. Shocked and terrified, he wrote in his diary that day:

Charles II, King of England, Scotland, and Ireland from 1649 to 1685. Charles II became unpopular after the Great Fire of London, which he mishandled. However, his reign remains relevant, because Prince William, who in 2007 was second in line to ascend the throne, is his descendant.

God grant mine eyes may never behold the like, who now saw above 10,000 houses all in one flame! The noise and cracking and thunder of the impetuous flames, the shrieking of women and children, the hurry of people, the fall of towers, houses, and churches, was like a hideous storm; and the air all about so hot and inflamed,

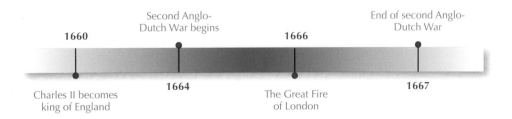

Second Anglo-Dutch War begins

End of second Anglo-Dutch War

1660

1666

1664

1667

Charles II becomes king of England

The Great Fire of London

that at the last one was not able to approach it, so that they were forced to stand still, and let the flames burn on, which they did, for near two miles in length and one in breadth.[3]

John Evelyn, 1620–1706. Evelyn was a well-known English author at the time of the Great Fire. He kept detailed diaries of important current events, including the burning of London.

Charles became increasingly desperate. He ordered his brother James, the Duke of York, to curb the chaos and organize firefighting efforts. Makeshift command posts soon surrounded the fire, and James offered lots of money to lower-class men to control the fire. Using long hooks, bands of newly minted firefighters demolished many buildings in an attempt to create a firebreak.

Not even their desperate efforts could prevent the fire from advancing westward toward Whitehall Palace, where Charles lived. During the early morning hours of Tuesday, September 4, James and his band of firefighters stood watch at the River Fleet, praying that the river would douse the flames. But the flames jumped the river and quickly surrounded the men on two sides. They fled, barely escaping with their lives. To the north, a man-made firebreak barely slowed down the flames. In the late afternoon the fire leaped over it to ravage the opulent shops lining Cheapside, one of London's most important streets. The Tower of London, which contained gunpowder stores, was also directly in the line of the fire. Had not firefighters successfully blocked the

1087

First Anglo-Dutch War begins

1654

Construction starts on
St. Paul's Cathedral

1652

First Anglo-Dutch War ends

Entrance to the River Fleet, painted by Samuel Scott around 1750. Nearly 100 years after the Great Fire of London, the city was bustling again. Its wooden buildings had been replaced by sturdier structures.

flames by blowing up houses near the Tower, the gunpowder would have exploded in a huge ball of flame.

Enormous chunks of London had fallen prey to the Great Fire. But, Londoners reasoned, the flames had eaten through wooden structures. Therefore, St. Paul's Cathedral, with its thick stone walls, should be fireproof. Using this logic, countless residents trekked to the cathedral, storing their belongings in its nooks and crannies. They did not take into account that the cathedral, now nearly 600 years old, was under repair. The scaffolding that fronted the building was tinder-dry wood. On Tuesday night, the scaffolding caught fire. Soon the lead roof began to melt. The molten liquid ran down the street. Books stored in the cathedral's crypt went up with a loud swoosh, and stones flew from the building.[4]

As St. Paul's Cathedral melted to the ground, the wind began to die down. The firebreaks around the fire's perimeter finally began to work. By

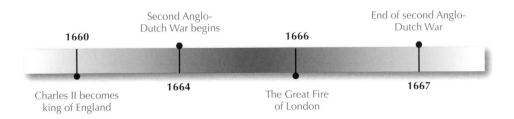

Second Anglo-Dutch War begins

End of second Anglo-Dutch War

1660

1666

1664

1667

Charles II becomes king of England

The Great Fire of London

St. Paul's Cathedral before the Great Fire of London. While the newer cathedral is still grand, it is smaller than the original.

Wednesday morning, September 5, flames were guttering and going out. Small fires still crackled here and there, but most of London was a smoking husk. Nearly all government buildings, thousands of houses, and almost 100 parish churches smoldered. Well over half of London's estimated half-million citizens—mostly the poor and middle-class—were left homeless. Many had erected makeshift shelters in a large public park. Others walked aimlessly around the smoldering streets, not knowing what to do next. According to official figures, only a few people—one of them Farriner's unfortunate maid—had died in the blaze. Others believe that many more perished, but their bodies had been completely consumed.[5]

People were devastated, angry, and looking for someone to blame. Conspiracy theories flew through the streets. Native-born Londoners looked suspiciously at foreigners, especially French and Dutch immigrants. The French were longtime political enemies, and at the time of the fire, England was involved in the Second Anglo-Dutch War. The Dutch, according to rumor-mongers, wanted to cripple England so that they could control European trade.

1087

First Anglo-Dutch War begins

1654

Construction starts on St. Paul's Cathedral

1652

First Anglo-Dutch War ends

More and more people began to think that "sneaky foreigners" had set the fires, hoping to drive honest Englishmen and women out of their homes and businesses. Many claimed to have seen such people lobbing manmade firebombs into thatched roofs. Furious mobs formed, beating anyone who looked suspicious; that is, anyone speaking French or Dutch.

One unfortunate young Frenchman—Robert Hubert—"confessed" to the crime. He could barely speak English, and was probably tortured. He was hanged a few weeks later. Soon afterward, a sea captain came forward and said that Hubert had been aboard his ship at the time of the fire.[6]

The eagerness to hang Hubert was a reflection of long-term animosity among the English, French, and Dutch. The English had won the first Anglo-Dutch War in 1654, but had not succeeded in driving the Dutch out of the world market. When Charles II ascended the throne in 1660, he helped to whip British citizens into a frenzy of anti-Dutch sentiment. Everybody who could read got their hands on pamphlets that detailed Dutch atrocities against the English.

The Great Fire of London was thus not just a fire. For thousands of Londoners who lost their homes, and for countless other Britons who hated the French and Dutch, it was a fearsome blaze designed to bring down the great power of England. While the city was eventually rebuilt, the legacy of the Great Fire lived on. As John Evelyn observed, "The conflagration was so universal, and the people so astonished that . . . there was nothing heard, or seen, but crying out and lamentation."[7]

The Great Fire of London was an unfortunate accident. But the underlying political tensions were not. They were typical of what had been going on for many years in Western Europe. The map of the continent had been undergoing changes for centuries before the fire. It would continue to change many times after that.

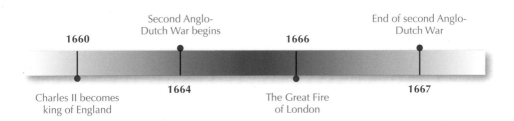

1660 — Charles II becomes king of England

Second Anglo-Dutch War begins — 1664

1666 — The Great Fire of London

End of second Anglo-Dutch War — 1667

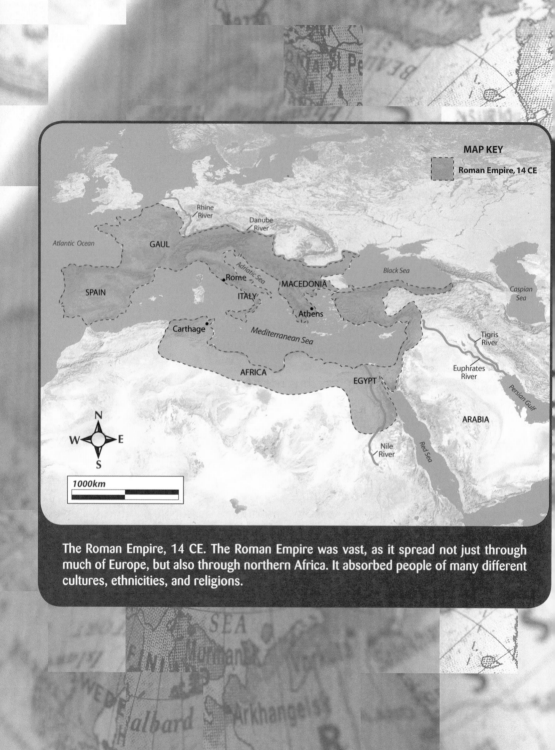

The Roman Empire, 14 CE. The Roman Empire was vast, as it spread not just through much of Europe, but also through northern Africa. It absorbed people of many different cultures, ethnicities, and religions.

The Rise and Fall of Rome

London owed its name and its founding in 43 CE to the Romans. The city was one of many outposts for the Romans, whose civilization dominated Western Europe for nearly a millennium. It transformed the European landscape from a collection of small tribal groups to an ever-expanding empire.

For more than two centuries after the Estruscan Empire was established around 750 BCE, Romans reluctantly functioned under the rule of the Etruscans, who dominated northern Italy. The Romans finally revolted in 509 BCE, drove the monarchy from power, and founded the Roman Republic.

The Roman Senate governed the republic in a relatively democratic form. Its consuls, or leaders, were elected. These elected officials were patricians, or members of the Roman aristocracy. Roman plebeians—merchants, farmers, workers and others—were not well represented in the government. Despite internal quarrels, however, Romans banded together against their enemies.

From 343 BCE to 146 BCE, Rome was almost continuously—and usually successfully—at war. First, Rome took control of the Italian peninsula. The people they conquered provided new recruits for the Roman army, which then spent more than a century engaged in the Punic Wars, a series of three conflicts against the northern African kingdom of Carthage. Rome finally destroyed Carthage, emerging as the leading power in the Mediterranean.

This victory gave way to a century of unrest. Rome's leaders pushed the borders they controlled further and further. Patricians profited from Rome's successes, while plebeians suffered. Because Rome was almost continuously at war, many plebeians spent most of their time fighting and little time working their land. As a result, they lost their land to patricians, who had gained slaves during wartime to work it.[1]

The ruins of Carthage, an ancient city on the northern border of Africa. It was a trading post for Phoenicians, also called Punics. Carthage was destroyed in 146 BCE.

Struggles between the two sides increased. Leaders rose and fell. A brief period of relative stability began in 60 BCE. Three of the most powerful men in Rome—Julius Caesar, Pompey the Great, and Marcus Crassus—formed the First Triumvirate (try-UM-vuh-rut, which means literally "three men"). Caesar championed the downtrodden plebeians and worked to return Rome to its republican roots. At the same time, he instigated the Gallic Wars (58–51 BCE) to expand Roman territory into Gaul. Eventually he annexed all of western mainland Europe. The Gallic Wars were gruesome and far-reaching; according to estimates, as many as 800 cities were conquered, three million people were killed in battle, and another million were sold into slavery.[2]

Start of the Roman Republic

750 BCE   343–146 BCE

Estruscans rule the Romans   509 BCE   Roman Republic expands borders

Vercingetorix throws down his arms at the feet of Julius Caesar. Vercingetorix was a Gallic leader who revolted against Caesar when Caesar tried to take over the Gauls. Unfortunately for the Gauls, Vercingetorix was unsuccessful.

By the time the Gallic Wars were over, the Triumvirate had fallen apart. Crassus was killed in battle in 53 BCE. Pompey became increasingly conservative and distanced himself from Caesar. Pompey even ordered Caesar to give up command of his army in 50 BCE. Caesar refused and led his army into a civil war against Pompey the following year. Pompey fled Rome, and Caesar and his army gave chase. Pompey sought safety in Egypt, but he was killed by the Egyptian pharaoh Ptolemy (TAHL-uh-mee) XIII in 48 BCE.

While Caesar was in Egypt, he became politically and romantically involved with the Egyptian queen Cleopatra. From Egypt, Caesar battled his

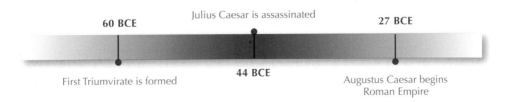

60 BCE

Julius Caesar is assassinated

27 BCE

First Triumvirate is formed

44 BCE

Augustus Caesar begins Roman Empire

way through the Middle East and northern Africa, gaining land and political supporters, before returning to Rome. He took much of the Senate's power into his own hands. Many of his fellow Romans revered him as a god. At the beginning of 44 BCE, he was appointed dictator for life.

Some important Romans thought that all this power was going to Caesar's head. His friend Marcus Brutus and other senators assassinated him on the Ides of March in 44 BCE.[3]

Caesar's death led to another civil war as his grandnephew Octavian formed the Second Triumvirate with Mark Antony and Lepidus. With Antony's help, Octavian quashed Caesar's assassins and booted Lepidus out of the Triumvirate.[4] Octavian then turned on Antony, who by then had become involved with Cleopatra, and defeated them in the Battle of Actium in 31 BCE.

Mort de Cesar, or *Death of Caesar,* a 1798 painting by Vincenzo Camuccini. Julius Caesar was assassinated on the Ides of March, or the middle of March. A clairvoyant predicted Caesar's death, but Caesar did not believe him.

Roman Empire reaches furthest extent

79 CE

284

Mt. Vesuvius erupts

117

Diocletian divides Roman Empire

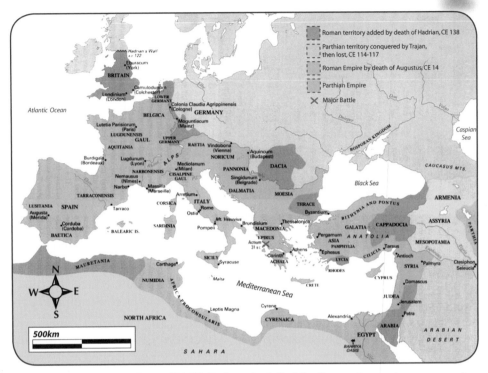

The Roman Empire, 14 CE to 476 CE. Before the fall of the Rome, its empire was growing in all directions. As it grew, so too did its influence over politics, religion, and trade.

Octavian absorbed Egypt into the territory controlled by Rome. In 27 BCE he took the name Augustus Caesar and became the first Roman emperor—and according to many historians, the greatest.[5] His reign ended the decades of civil conflict that had cost uncounted thousands of Romans their lives. It also ended the Roman Republic. From then on, Rome would be ruled by an emperor and be known as the Roman Empire.

330 — Emperor Constantine establishes Constantinople
410 — Visigoths sack Rome
476 — Fall of Western Roman Empire

Chapter 2

An artist's impression of Pompeii on its last day. Mount Vesuvius erupted in 79 CE, spewing lava and volcanic ash over the city. Pompeii stayed buried until archaeologists excavated it 1,700 years later.

The emperors following Augustus after his death in 14 CE were not as skilled. One of the worst was Nero, who supposedly "fiddled while Rome burned," a reference to a great fire that consumed much of Rome in 64. Four years later Nero committed suicide. An even more troubled period followed, including one year when Rome was ruled by four emperors. The natural world seemed to reflect this instability. The eruption of Mount Vesuvius, less than 100 miles from Rome, occurred in 79. The disaster buried the cities of Pompeii and Herculaneum in volcanic ash.

Rome regained its footing with the "Five Good Emperors," beginning with the brief reign of Nerva in 96. After Nerva's death two years later, Trajan used his extensive experience as a military commander to expand Rome's borders. By the time of his death in 117, the Roman Empire had reached its furthest extent. More than six decades of relative peace followed.

This period ended with the reign of Commodus, which ushered in a century of political instability until Diocletian (dye-oh-KLEE-shun) took power in 284. He divided the empire into eastern and western halves. The western empire soon declined in power. Beginning in 330, the seat of imperial power officially resided in the east, when Constantine established Constantinople to serve as the capital of the Roman Empire.[6]

Constantine's most notable successor, Theodosius I, made a final stab at ruling both east and west when he came to power in 392. But the western empire remained open to attack, especially after Theodosius died in 395. The Visigoths, a fierce tribe of barbarians, sacked Rome in 410. This led to the western empire's downfall in 476 when the Germanic chieftain Odoacer deposed Romulus Augustus, the last Roman emperor.[7]

Cleopatra, Queen of Egypt

Cleopatra became the queen of Egypt in 50 BCE at the age of eighteen. She was the country's joint ruler with her twelve-year-old brother (and later husband) Ptolemy XIII. Ptolemy soon exiled his sister-bride and seized power. But he botched Egypt's relationship with Rome. He ordered the murder of the Roman general Pompey, thinking that Julius Caesar would appreciate the death of his political opponent. Caesar was furious when Ptolemy presented Pompey's severed head to him. Cleopatra took her chance to regain power by appealing to Caesar, who helped her overthrow Ptolemy.[8]

She remained close to Caesar until his assassination. A savvy queen, Cleopatra wished to stay on good terms with the Romans. She delighted Mark Antony, one of Caesar's successors. She became his wife, and eventually bore him three children. The relationship between Cleopatra and Antony was as political as it was romantic. Their three children were crowned rulers of the eastern lands that Antony conquered. Most Romans were enraged because they felt that Antony had no right to give away Roman lands to the children of a non-Roman queen.

The Death of Cleopatra, painted around 1914. Cleopatra's dramatic story continues to fascinate people around the world. Many films have been made and books written about her life and tragic death.

As a result, Octavian waged war against Antony and Cleopatra. In the confusion after being defeated at the battle of Actium, Antony heard that his beloved Cleopatra had committed suicide. Devastated, Antony killed himself. In fact, the rumors about Cleopatra's death were false. She was alive, though a prisoner of Octavian. Grief-stricken when she learned of Antony's demise, she ordered two handmaidens to bring her a venomous asp in a basket of figs. According to Roman historian Plutarch, "[W]hen she took away some of the figs and saw it, she said, 'So here it is,' and held out her bare arm to be bitten."[9] Cleopatra, as well as her two loyal handmaidens, perished. The relationship that Cleopatra had cultivated with the Roman Empire was over, as was the reign of the pharaohs. From then on Egypt would be a province of the Roman Empire rather than an independent country.[10]

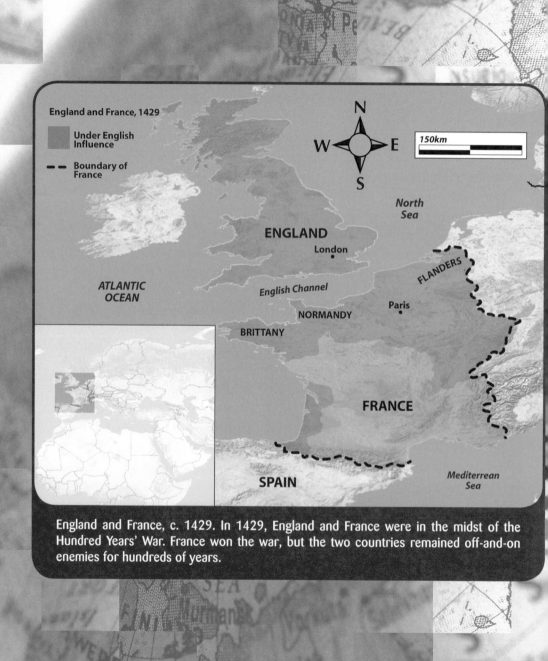

England and France, 1429

Under English Influence

- - Boundary of France

150km

N
W E
S

North Sea

ENGLAND

London

ATLANTIC OCEAN

English Channel

NORMANDY

BRITTANY

FLANDERS

Paris

FRANCE

SPAIN

Mediterrean Sea

England and France, c. 1429. In 1429, England and France were in the midst of the Hundred Years' War. France won the war, but the two countries remained off-and-on enemies for hundreds of years.

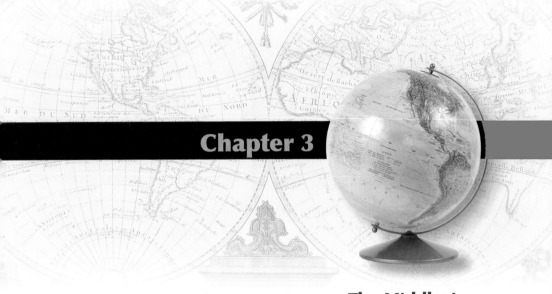

Chapter 3

The Middle Ages

Even before Rome fell in 476, the western empire was changing into a smattering of provincial kingdoms and tribal states. The Christian Church became the primary unifying force. This unity was most effective in Gaul, the region that Caesar had invaded several centuries earlier. The Franks, a conglomeration of several Germanic tribes, had migrated there. They combined their tribal traditions with Roman ways to create a society called Francia.[1]

In 732, Frankish ruler Charles Martel defeated an invading Islamic army at the Battle of Tours. Many historians believe this battle determined that Europe would continue to develop under Christianity rather than Islam.

Charles's grandson Charlemagne (Charles the Great) became even more famous as he extended Frankish control over nearly all of Western Europe. In 800, Pope Leo III crowned Charlemagne as "Emperor of the Romans."[2] It was a clear sign that the memory of the Western Roman Empire was still very much alive even though it had fallen more than 300 years earlier.

This period also marked the rise of a feudal system in which lords owned all the land upon which serfs, or peasants, worked. Lords generally treated their serfs almost like slaves, but gave them housing, food, and protection from traveling bandits or troops from other areas. Between lords and serfs were soldiers who swore allegiance to a particular lord. These soldiers often became knights, who held themselves to a high standard of ethics called chivalry.[3]

The order that Charlemagne established began to fragment at his death in 814. In the next 200 years, small kingdoms achieved new heights; specifically the Franks, the Saxons in England, the Ostrogoths in Italy, and the Visigoths in Spain and Portugal.[4]

The High Middle Ages, which began around the year 1000, saw a revitalization of centralized authority and stability in Western Europe. Farmers grew larger crops, people were well fed and healthier, and many serfs worked their way up to the merchant class. Wealthy merchants founded libraries and universities, including the University of Paris in 1150. Intellectual and artistic culture grew with advances in sculpture, music, and architecture.

Charles Martel and the Battle of Tours, painted by Charles de Steuben. In October 732, the Frankish ruler Charles Martel repelled Muslim invaders from Spain. This was called the Battle of Tours, and took place in the northwestern section of modern-day France.

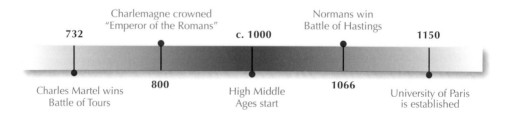

Charlemagne crowned "Emperor of the Romans"

c. 1000

Normans win Battle of Hastings

732

1150

Charles Martel wins Battle of Tours

800

High Middle Ages start

1066

University of Paris is established

Moreover, instead of thinking of themselves in terms of their feudal lords or small kingdoms, people began to think of themselves in terms of their countries. The more powerful countries fought for supremacy. In 1066, the Normans, who were from France, defeated an English army at the Battle of Hastings. The invasion was led by William the Conqueror, the Duke of Normandy. William installed a powerful Norman monarchy in England, tying it more closely to Western Europe. However, it also began an animosity between France and England that would last for centuries.[5]

England flourished under Norman control. For example, King Henry II controlled Normandy and Anjou as his birthright, and gained Touraine, Aquitaine, and Gascony when he married Eleanor of Aquitaine in 1152. After he ascended the throne in 1154, Henry turned his attention to Ireland. Within two decades, he became the Lord of Ireland. For the next nearly eight centuries, England dominated Ireland.

King Charlemagne of the Franks. Charlemagne was a devout Catholic who maintained close ties to the papacy. After his death, Antipope Paschal III canonized Charlemagne as a saint, but his sainthood was soon revoked.

By the end of the twelfth century, England had extensive landholdings and a powerful monarchy. Starting in the early thirteenth century, King John of England curtailed England's success. He challenged the authority of the church, raised taxes, and lost lands in France that had been under English control.

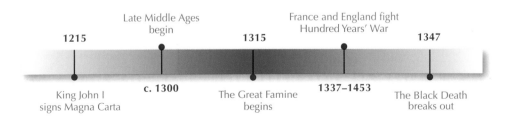

1215	Late Middle Ages begin	1315	France and England fight Hundred Years' War	1347
King John I signs Magna Carta	c. 1300	The Great Famine begins	1337–1453	The Black Death breaks out

In 1215, dissatisfied English noblemen known as barons forced King John to sign the "Articles of the Barons." This event was recorded in a formal document, which became known as the Magna Carta ("Great Charter"). It was designed to check the power of the king so that he could not abuse it as John had.[6]

The prosperity that had characterized Western Europe during the High Middle Ages faded at the beginning of the fourteenth century. Historians call this century and the one that followed the Late Middle Ages. During the first half of the 1300s, Europe underwent an economic and demographic upheaval. Inflation had been building since the eleventh century, and it spun out of control in the early part of the fourteenth century.

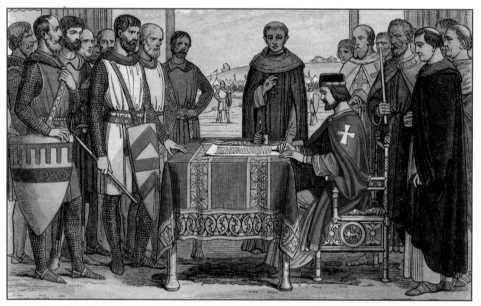

King John signs the Magna Carta (Latin for "Great Charter"). King John signed the document in 1215 to reach peace in England. Many important documents, including the American Bill of Rights, are based on the Magna Carta.

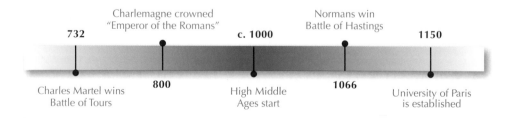

Charlemagne crowned
"Emperor of the Romans"

Normans win
Battle of Hastings

732

c. 1000

1150

Charles Martel wins
Battle of Tours

800

High Middle
Ages start

1066

University of Paris
is established

Added to this instability were malnutrition and disease. The Great Famine, for example, killed millions of people all over Europe between 1315 and 1317 and weakened many more. Affecting northern Europe, including the relatively wealthy England, the famine hit at a time when the population of Europe was at an unprecedented high. A few years of unrelenting bad weather crippled wheat harvests, food prices rose sharply, and ineffective local governments found themselves powerless to feed their people. While the poor were the hardest hit, even King Edward II of England found himself without food on one occasion.[7] Soon thereafter, the Black Death further devastated Europe, killing up to one-third of the population.

Conditions became even more chaotic in the fifteenth century. The feudal system broke down and religious differences arose. The lower social orders no longer felt the need to work for higher social classes in exchange for protection. Indeed, several peasant uprisings took place during the Late Middle Ages. Because so many peasants died during the plague years, there was suddenly more land and less cheap labor to work on it. Landowners began competing for workers by offering unprecedented incentives. Many peasants moved from place to place to earn a better living.[8]

Joan of Arc at the Siege of Orleans, part of the Hundred Years' War. Despite the war's name, it lasted well over a hundred years. However, there were long period of calm between battles.

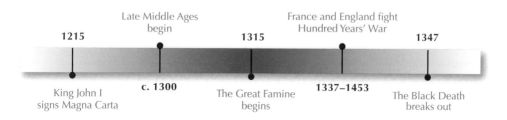

1215	Late Middle Ages begin	**1315**	France and England fight Hundred Years' War	**1347**
King John I signs Magna Carta	**c. 1300**	The Great Famine begins	**1337–1453**	The Black Death breaks out

Joan at the Coronation of Charles VII, painted by Jean August Dominique Ingres in 1854. This painting shows Joan of Arc in skirts. However, she usually dressed in men's clothing.

Developing nations experienced growing pains. This was apparent in conflicts like the Hundred Years' War, which ran from 1337 to 1453 as England and France fought over the right to the French throne. Early on, France suffered both physical and economic devastation. By the early 1400s, England was well on its way to establishing an English-controlled dual monarchy. Aided by Joan of Arc, the French recovered and eventually successfully drove the English from their country.[9]

In short, much of Europe was laid to waste by political and religious conflicts, economic decline, and disease during the Middle Ages. With devastation, though, came a new Europe, one that encouraged a strong sense of national identity and valued science and the arts. The Renaissance was on the horizon.

The Black Death

The Black Death, one of the worst plagues in European history, started in October 1347. Most of the sailors manning a fleet traveling from Kaffa (in modern-day Russia) to the Italian city of Messina died of a horrible disease. It began with a headache and chills. Soon the men suffered from bright red blotches and swollen lumps on their chests. The lumps turned black and burst. By then they were vomiting blood, cough-

The Black Death, as illustrated in the Toggenburg Bible in 1411. The Black Death, or bubonic plague, was characterized by buboes, lumps on the skin that could get as large as an orange. Plagues recurred several times in Europe.

ing and sneezing. Almost all died within a few days of contracting the disease.

Some ships lost all their men and ran aground, where they were looted. The looters, in turn, transmitted the disease on land. Soon the plague spread to Genoa and Venice. In 1348, writer Gabriele de' Mussi lamented the effects of the Black Death on the Italian population. "Alas!" he cried. "Our ships enter the port, but of a thousand sailors hardly ten are spared. We reach our homes; our kindred and our neighbors come from all parts to visit us. . . . Whilst we spoke to them, whilst they embraced us and kissed us, we scattered the poison from our lips. Going back to their homes, they in turn soon infected their whole families, who in three days succumbed, and were buried in one common grave. Priests and doctors visiting the sick returned from their duties ill, and soon were numbered with the dead."[10]

The Black Death continued its ravages. Within a few months, France, Spain, Portugal, and England fell victim to the disease. Between 1348 and 1350, the plague laid waste to Germany and Scandinavia, then moved on to Russia.

Fourteenth-century Europeans could only guess how the Black Death was spread. Because the plague spread along trade routes, Europeans thought that exported grains, fish, and other foodstuffs might carry the disease. They didn't realize it, but the disease was actually spread by infected rats and fleas. Neverthe-less, many leaders banned exports, isolating countries from each other and contributing to widespread economic recession.

By 1352 the worst of the plague was over. It would return numerous times in the following centuries.

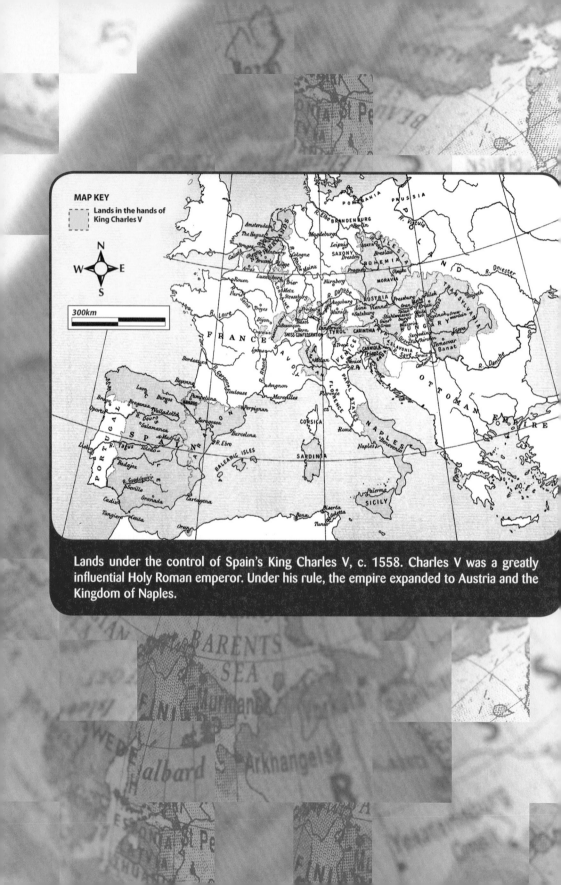

MAP KEY

Lands in the hands of King Charles V

N
W E
S

300km

Lands under the control of Spain's King Charles V, c. 1558. Charles V was a greatly influential Holy Roman emperor. Under his rule, the empire expanded to Austria and the Kingdom of Naples.

Chapter 4

The Golden Age

In the Middle Ages, Europeans were primarily concerned with day-to-day survival in primitive circumstances and the teachings of the Church. As this era began to fade, the upper classes of Europe laid the groundwork for a more modern time.

This period is known as the Renaissance (REH-nuh-zants), which means "rebirth." It refers to a rebirth of art and learning that began in Italy and had the biggest impact there. In the Late Middle Ages, key northern Italian cities began developing into political and economic powerhouses. These cities received wool, wheat, and other goods from France and Germany. They also stood between the eastern and western worlds. On the coast, the cities of Genoa, Pisa, and Venice benefited from trade with countries that lay far to the east. In turn, the Italians sold these eastern luxury goods—like spices and silks—throughout Europe.[1]

Trade goods weren't all that came into Italy. Artists and scholars were inspired by knowledge and texts available through the same trade routes. Works of the ancient Greeks and Romans had been trickling into Europe from Arabic countries for several centuries. Italian intellectuals revered these works and reviled the Middle Ages.

This trickle began a torrent in 1453 when Muslim armies captured Constantinople, which marked the end of the Eastern Roman Empire.[2] Many Christian scholars fled to Italy and brought even more ancient works with them.

The road to the Renaissance, however, was bumpy. The Black Death of the mid-1300s had decimated the population in major Italian cities. While nobody was immune to the plague, most of the people who died were poor.

A modern image of Venice. The city, central to the Italian Renaissance, is built on rivers and lagoons. Its nicknames include the City of Water and the City of Bridges.

They lived in close quarters in especially unsanitary conditions. As a result, many people who survived were of the wealthier classes. They had the time, education, and money to participate in international trade, the arts, and science. They also witnessed the Church's inability to slow the brutal progress of the plague, and started questioning its teachings and influence. Many believed in humanism, a philosophy that emphasized personal experience rather than church teachings.

Wealthy residents of cities like Florence such as the Medicis (MEH-duh-cheez), a family of merchant bankers, began supporting artists and scholars. Many of the most famous names in cultural history emerged during this time: the sculptor Michelangelo, the author Machiavelli, the painter Botticelli, and

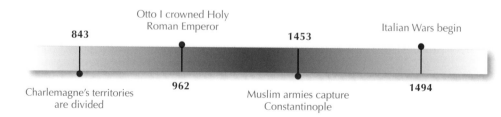

Otto I crowned Holy
Roman Emperor
843   1453   Italian Wars begin

Charlemagne's territories   962   Muslim armies capture   1494
are divided   Constantinople

the true Renaissance man (because he did so much in so many different fields) Leonardo da Vinci.[3]

The Renaissance spread from Florence to other Italian cities. Renaissance architecture flourished in Venice. In 1443, Alfonso I took over Naples and drew artists, writers, and philosophers. Four years later, Milan became an artistic and cultural mecca under the rule of Francesco Sforza. That same year, Rome received a much-needed boost from the newly elected Pope Nicholas V. Many buildings of the ancient city had fallen into ruin, so Nicholas began an ambitious program of reconstruction. Subsequent popes instilled Renaissance art and philosophies into the papacy.[4]

The Medici family, portrayed by Sandro Botticelli in the *Madonna del Magnificat*. The Medicis, who were patrons of the arts, sponsored Botticelli. A Florentine painter, Botticelli completed one of his most famous works, *The Birth of Venus*, in 1486.

Italians may have felt secure in their intellectual accomplishments, but they were far from secure in domestic and international affairs. The cities all had standing armies made up of mercenaries, or soldiers who fought for whoever would pay them. These cities continually pitted their armies against each other as they vied for dominance. The incessant fighting weakened them, and the ideals of the Renaissance began to decline.

Foreign invasions, in the form of the Italian Wars, delivered the final blows. Nearly all of Western Europe was involved, with France and Spain the main contenders. France started the conflict in 1494, when King Charles VIII invaded Italy. An often bewildering series of battles, betrayals, alliances, and counteralliances followed for more than six decades. The conflict ended

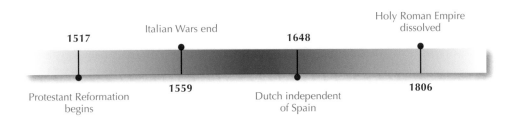

1517 — Protestant Reformation begins

Italian Wars end — 1559

1648 — Dutch independent of Spain

Holy Roman Empire dissolved — 1806

in 1559, with Spain emerging triumphant. The important Italian cities of the Renaissance were decimated. It would be more than three centuries before they would be united into a single country.[5]

The Italian Renaissance influenced other major European countries, which flourished both commercially and culturally in a "golden age." Major figures such as Leonardo da Vinci left an increasingly unstable Italy to live

Statue of Michelangelo, who was famous during and after his lifetime for his prolific artwork. Two of his most famous pieces are the statue *David* and the ceiling of the Sistine Chapel.

Statue of Leonardo da Vinci. Leonardo wore many hats during his lifetime, working as an artist, architect, and musician, among other occupations. Two of his best-known works are the paintings *Mona Lisa* and *The Last Supper*.

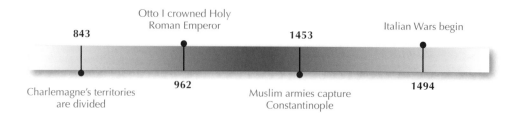

Otto I crowned Holy Roman Emperor

843

1453

Italian Wars begin

Charlemagne's territories are divided

962

Muslim armies capture Constantinople

1494

elsewhere, and travelers soaked up some of the spirit of the Renaissance.[6] Moreover, foreign armies that had invaded Italy came home with more than plunder; they also brought an interest in art and science. While the Renaissance periods of Germany, the Netherlands, and England drew from their Italian predecessor, they were unique in many ways.

In Germany and the Netherlands, Renaissance ideals undergirded a desire for religious and political change. In 1517, German monk Martin Luther called for the reformation of the Church in a tract entitled *95 Theses on the Power of Indulgences Criticizing the Church*. Many people, who became known as Protestants, supported Luther's criticisms. Protestants believed that everybody, and not just the learned clergy, should be able to read the Bible. With the invention of the printing press, more people got their own Bibles. The Protestant Reformation quickly divided

Martin Luther as painted by Lucas Cranach in 1529. Luther was married and had six children. He had a reputation for being argumentative and an egomaniac.

Europe religiously. It resulted in numerous persecutions and wars as Protestants and Catholics battled each other fiercely.

Renaissance thinking also supported a desire for political independence. Germany and the Netherlands were governed not only by local rulers, but

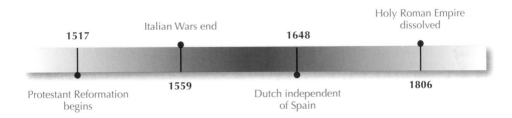

Holy Roman Empire
dissolved

1517

Italian Wars end

1648

Protestant Reformation
begins

1559

Dutch independent
of Spain

1806

William of Orange, also known as William III of England. After an illustrious political career, William fell off his horse and died in 1702.

also by Holy Roman Emperor and Spanish king Charles V. Charles was a Catholic, so the Protestant-leaning northern Europeans formed alliances against him. In the 1530s and 1540s, Charles moved to suppress these dissenters, most notably through the Spanish Inquisition, which tried and executed many non-Catholics.[7] Charles's son and successor Phillip II continued his father's brutal legacy. In response, William, Prince of Orange, sought to release the Netherlands' southern and northern provinces from Spanish control. Though unsuccessful, William inspired a tense peace between Spain and the Netherlands in the mid-1580s. Soon thereafter, prosperity reigned in the Netherlands, and in 1648, Spain finally declared the Dutch independent. But internal disunity led the Dutch into a series of devastating wars with England that began in 1652. By the time they ended more than three decades later, warfare had devastated the Dutch and elevated the English to rulers of the sea.[8]

The Holy Roman Empire

Charlemagne's coronation in 800 as "Emperor of the Romans" was an effort to maintain the existence of the Roman Empire. His son Louis tried to hold his father's empire together, but he wasn't strong enough. After Louis's death in 843, the vast territories that Charlemagne had controlled were split into several smaller areas. One of these, consisting of much of modern-day Germany, was eventually ruled by Otto I, who was crowned emperor by Pope John XII in 962.[9] Historians regard this date as the beginning of the Holy Roman Empire, although it didn't receive this name officially for several centuries. It was called "Holy" because of its connection with the Church.

At first, the popes and the emperors worked well together. Just over a century later, a struggle for power emerged between the two sides. By the middle of the thirteenth century, the empire had taken the form it would assume for the following centuries, a changing collection of territories and nations in Central Europe. Although the Empire occupied more territory than any other country in that area, most of the power resided with the rulers of the smaller nations that composed. It still remained a powerful player in European politics until about 1650.

A century later, the French philosopher François-Marie Arouet de Voltaire summed up the situation of the Holy Roman Empire as "neither Holy, nor Roman, nor an Empire."[10] It didn't have a capital or a central administration, most of the people under its control were Germans, and its religious connections were very loose. It lasted until 1806 when it was dissolved by the French emperor Napoleon Bonaparte.[11]

In reality, therefore, the Holy Roman Empire bore little resemblance to the original other than lasting nearly a thousand years. While the Holy Roman Empire fell hard, it had once been a major contender on the European stage.

The Holy Roman Empire was key to the formation of a modern Europe.

ATLANTIC
OCEAN

Santo
Domingo
(Sp.)

St.
Domingue
(Fr.)

Caribbean Sea

Guadeloupe 1759
Dominica 1761
Martinique 1761
St. Lucia 1762
St. Vincent 1762

Grenada 1762

French
territory

British
capture

•

ATLANTIC
OCEAN

Great Lakes

Louisbourg
1758

Quebec
1759

Braddock's
defeat
1755

Havana
1762

Cuba (Sp.)

British territory

French territory

British capture
or victory

French capture
or victory

British and French territories and battles during the Seven Years' War, 1754–1763. Both England and France scrambled to claim as much territory as possible in the New World and elsewhere.

Chapter 5

The Old Regime Turns New

As Renaissance ideals continued to spread in the sixteenth and seventeenth centuries, Europeans began to question the world around them. This questioning led to the Scientific Revolution. The number of Europeans who held on to the old superstitious beliefs like witchcraft was declining.[1]

Changes in thinking led to changes in society during the eighteenth century. These changes, however, were slow in coming. With the exception of Great Britain, Western Europe was accustomed to operating under the Old Regime, which consisted of societies led by strong monarchs. These monarchs were supported by growing bureaucracies and powerful armies and navies. Below the monarch were common people, most of whom lived their entire lives in the social class into which they were born.

Many people began to experience lifestyle changes during the early and middle eighteenth century. As the population of Europe grew, an increasing number of farmers grew food not just for their families and communities, but also for larger domestic and international markets.[2]

To further enrich themselves, Western Europe's three most powerful countries—Great Britain, France, and Spain—colonized lands beyond their own continent that were rich with natural resources. The increasingly sophisticated transatlantic trade routes became a source of great profit for Europe's major players. The British controlled North America's eastern seaboard and the islands of Bermuda, Jamaica, and Barbados. France claimed major North American routes along the Saint Lawrence, Ohio, and Mississippi Rivers, as well as Guadeloupe, Martinique, and modern-day Haiti in the Caribbean Sea. Spain dominated Mexico, California, Florida, and the American Southwest in addition to Cuba, Puerto Rico, Trinidad, the modern-day Dominican

Republic and most of South America. The Dutch, Swedish and Portuguese also had some holdings.

In large part, the expansion of these overseas empires drove the major European powers to battle each other for supremacy. The French and British, who already had a tense relationship, continuously squabbled over their holdings in North America and the West Indies.[3] Not surprisingly, the mid-eighteenth century became a period of intense warfare among European nations.

A spate of conflicts kicked off with the War of Jenkins' Ear. By 1730, Spain was trying to monopolize all trade with the West Indies, which led to a great deal of smuggling and other illegal activities by the British. In 1731, a Spanish patrol boarded a British ship commanded by Robert Jenkins and cut off his ear. Jenkins had the foresight (or a grisly sense of humor) to pickle his ear in a jar of brandy, and presented it to Parliament in 1738. This dramatic incident prompted Britain to declare war on Spain in 1739. It lasted until 1742, at which point it became part of the much larger War of the Austrian Succession.

This conflict began in 1740 when Prussia's new king Frederick II (who later became known as Frederick the Great) captured the province of Silesia in eastern Germany. Up to that point, Silesia had been part of the Hapsburg Empire, which had arisen several centuries earlier and was now centered in modern-day Austria. A new empress, Maria Theresa, had just taken the throne. Other rulers thought she would be weak because she was a woman.

Rather than allow her rivals to seize other Hapsburg holdings, Maria Theresa kept her empire together. To secure the loyalty of her Hungarian subjects, she granted the country's nobility greater independence than the rulers of other Hapsburg territories. France then jumped into the conflict, supporting the Prussians against Austria, France's longtime enemy. Afraid that France would get the upper hand, Britain joined the Austrian forces against Prussia.

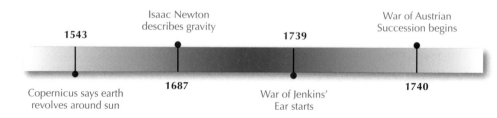

1543	Isaac Newton describes gravity	1739	War of Austrian Succession begins
Copernicus says earth revolves around sun	1687	War of Jenkins' Ear starts	1740

The Battle of Fontenoy, a key battle in the War of the Austrian Succession. The war involved many major European powers. People in North America referred to it as King George's War.

In 1748, the war ended with the Treaty of Aix-la-Chapelle, wherein Prussia kept Silesia.[4]

Europe settled into a period of relative peace, though it didn't last very long. In 1756, the temperamental Frederick started the Seven Years' War. It quickly spilled over into North America with the French and Indian War, which pitted England against France.[5]

Both conflicts ended in 1763. While the Seven Years' War resulted in little change in the borders of the antagonists, the situation was very different

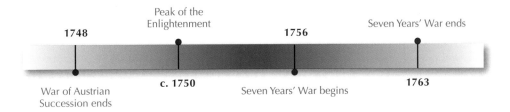

Peak of the Enlightenment

1748

1756

Seven Years' War ends

c. 1750

Seven Years' War begins

1763

War of Austrian Succession ends

in North America. Britain squashed the French and took over almost all of France's North American territory.[6]

War was not the only thing occupying the minds of Europeans during the eighteenth century. Just as they had during the Scientific Revolution of the previous two centuries, intellectuals felt the need to make sense of their world. This drive surfaced in the Enlightenment, a wide-ranging movement based on the idea that human reason could be used to build a better world.

Frederick II at age sixty-eight, by Anton Graff. Also known as Frederick the Great, this king was interested in the arts from an early age. His father, the fearsome Frederick William I, discouraged such pursuits.

Empress Maria Theresa of Austria bucked all convention when she assumed empress duties for the Holy Roman Empire. During her reign, she improved Austria's agriculture, educational system, and army.

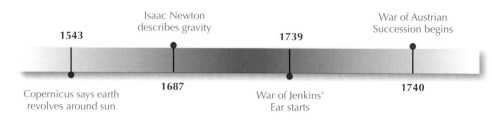

1543

Copernicus says earth revolves around sun

Isaac Newton describes gravity

1687

1739

War of Jenkins' Ear starts

War of Austrian Succession begins

1740

The Battle of Kunersdorff, painted in 1848 by Alexander Kotzebue. The battle was part of the Seven Years' War, which engaged a wide range of nations and territories. Fought on many fronts, it was the first truly global war.

While its origins went back many years, it reached its peak about 1750 with thinkers such as the Baron de Montesquieu (1689–1755), François-Marie Arouet de Voltaire (1694–1766), David Hume (1711–1776), Jean-Jacques Rousseau (1712–1788), and Adam Smith (1723–1790).

Many Europeans tried to translate Enlightenment beliefs into a practical reality. In the Old Regime, the rigid social system went largely unchallenged. According to the concept of divine right, God had literally granted the monarch of a country the power over its citizens. Enlightenment thinkers brought

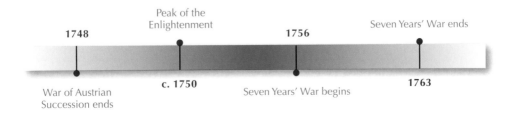

1748

War of Austrian
Succession ends

Peak of the
Enlightenment

c. 1750

1756

Seven Years' War begins

Seven Years' War ends

1763

The Scot David Hume was an important figure in the Enlightenment. Among other things, he was a historian. He published a seminal work entitled *The History of England*.

Jean-Jacques Rousseau in his later years. Rousseau was both a popular and controversial figure during his lifetime.

forth the idea of natural law, under which a monarch's subjects had God-given rights of their own.[7] People began to think that individuals could have a larger voice in their governments, an idea that lies at the root of the modern-day concept of democracy.

But not all rulers were willing to go along with these new ideas. Frederick the Great, for example, believed that a strong state benefited its citizens. Without regulations and standards imposed from above, neighbors would fight neighbors, the economy would collapse, and anarchy would result.

In spite of opposition from rulers such as Frederick, more and more Europeans were affected by philosophical ideas as the eighteenth century wore on. Scientific theories and political philosophies were no longer just for great thinkers. Rather, Europeans of all stripes became familiar with them as the Old Regime turned new.

The Scientific Revolution

The Scientific Revolution arrived on the heels of the Renaissance. Astronomer Nicolaus Copernicus kicked off the revolution in 1543 when he published the highly controversial *On the Revolutions of the Heavenly Spheres*. In this work, Copernicus argued that the sun, not the earth, was the center of the universe. Copernicus was just the first in a network of scientists, philosophers, and other scholars who challenged the status quo.[8]

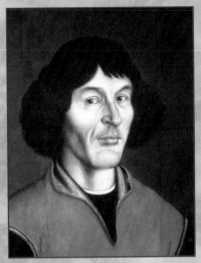

Nicolaus Copernicus

For many centuries, people believed the ideas of ancient thinkers such as Aristotle (AIR-uh-stah-tull). One was the concept of bodily humors. According to this concept, all humans had four humors, or fluids: blood, phlegm (FLEM), black bile, and yellow bile. Disease resulted when these humors became unbalanced. According to another idea, everything on earth was made out of just four elements: earth, air, fire and water.[9]

During the course of the Scientific Revolution, a spate of scientists, physicians, and philosophers began replacing time-honored ideas. Cutting-edge scientists influenced by Copernicus became convinced that the earth revolved around the sun instead of the other way around. Medical practitioners questioned the concept of bodily humors as they searched for the real causes of sickness. Still other thinkers argued that the earth's elements were much more complex than the original four.

At about the same time as Copernicus, Andreas Vesalius discovered that the function of the heart was to pump blood through the body. Just over a century later, Antony van Leeuwenhoek (LAY-ven-hook) developed a microscope that facilitated the study of medicine and biology. Sir Francis Bacon and Rene Descartes (ruh-NAY day-CART) studied how people think. Sir Isaac Newton added to the work of Johannes Kepler and Galileo, important figures of the earlier Scientific Revolution who in turn had built upon the work of Copernicus. Newton also developed calculus (a form of mathematics), and his 1687 book *Principia* described the theory of gravity. Modern science was indeed in the making.[10]

The Empire of Napoleon, 1810

ATLANTIC
OCEAN

North
Sea

Baltic
Sea

KINGDOM
OF NORWAY
AND
DENMARK

KINGDOM
OF
SWEDEN

GREAT
BRITAIN

• Moscow

Friedland
(1807)

PRUSSIA

Berlin

Leipzig
(1813)

GRAND DUCHY
OF WARSAW

Niemen R.

RUSSIAN   EMPIRE

London •

Brussels •

Amiens •

Waterloo
(1815)

CONFEDERATION

Jena (1806)

Kiev •

Versailles • • Paris

OF THE

Austerlitz
(1805)

Ulm
(1805)

RHINE

Wagram (1809)

Dniester River

Vienna

AUSTRIAN   EMPIRE

FRENCH
EMPIRE

Po

• Milan

River

Danube
River

Black   Sea

KINGDOM
OF
ITALY

PORTUGAL

Ebro River

Madrid •

Tagus R.

SPAIN

CORSICA

Rome •

OTTOMAN

Istanbul •

EMPIRE

SARDINIA

Naples •

KINGDOM
OF NAPLES

Trafalgar
(1805) • Gibraltar
(Br.)

MEDITERRANEAN   SEA

SICILY

KEY

- French empire
- Countries under Napoleon's control
- Countries allied with Napoleon
- Countries at war with Napoleon
- ✿ Battle

The Napoleonic Empire, 1810. Napoleon's empire grew rapidly throughout the first part of the nineteenth century. Although he was an egomaniac, Napoleon was a brilliant commander and inspired his troops to fight for French expansion.

Chapter 6

A Time of Revolution

The European Enlightenment was a bloodless revolution of ideas.[1] But the European wars centered around France that raged through the late eighteenth and early nineteenth centuries were just the opposite. The French Revolution and the Napoleonic Wars resulted in countless numbers of deaths.

The French Revolution resulted from internal political turmoil that had been festering since the middle of the eighteenth century. Enlightenment ideals—mainly republicanism—inspired frustrated French men and women. Republicanism, an idea that went back to ancient Rome, stressed that a country's people, not the monarchy, should be the ruling body. According to this idea, the government should exist to protect the liberty and equality of its citizens. It should not rule them arbitrarily or tax them heavily.[2]

By the late 1780s, the French economy was a disaster. Fighting the Seven Years' War and other conflicts had been very expensive. France was deeply in debt to other countries, and inflation was out of control. The economic gap between a relatively small number of wealthy people and the desperately poor peasants was widening. Many peasants couldn't even afford to buy bread. Most French people considered King Louis XVI and his queen Marie Antoinette incompetent and corrupt. Louis made things worse by levying heavy taxes on his subjects in an attempt to pay down the French debt and finance the monarchy.

The Revolution officially began on July 14, 1789, a date still celebrated today in France as Bastille Day. A Parisian mob marched on royal troops in a fortress called the Bastille. The troops fired into the oncoming crowd, which still managed to storm the fortress and slaughter some of the defenders.

The storming of the Bastille. Upon hearing about the incident, King Louis XVI supposedly asked, "Is this a revolt?" He was told, "No, Sire, it is a revolution."

This set the stage for a long and bloody conflict that resulted in radical changes. Peasants rose up against nobility, the feudal system toppled, and starving city-dwellers rioted. In 1791, France became a constitutional monarchy with the formation of the Legislative Assembly that ran the country with a little help from the king. When the Legislative Assembly fragmented, Louis and his family tried to flee but were quickly captured. Louis was tried and convicted for conspiring against liberty. He went to the guillotine in January of 1793, and his wife soon followed.[3]

French Revolution begins

1774

1793

Napoleon becomes emperor of France

1789

Louis XVI becomes French king

Louis XVI, Marie Antoinette guillotined

1804

King Louis XVI, age twenty, just after he ascended the throne.

Not everyone in France supported the Revolution. Some anti-Revolution citizens attacked their own country's troops. These counterrevolutionaries suffered at the hands of Maximilien Robespierre, a Revolutionary leader who established the Revolutionary Tribunal. Under the tribunal, France experienced the Reign of Terror from April 1793 to May 1794. During this bloody year, the tribunal sent 2,750 people to the guillotine.[4] This number paled, though, in comparison to the 40,000 people executed by smaller tribunals during the winter of 1793 and 1794.[5] Robespierre himself went to the guillotine in 1795. After his death, France formed the *Directoire* to run the country.

Other countries watched in horror as violence raged through France; they hoped to quash the French Revolution. Incensed, France began a series of wars. Their efforts would have been doomed but for the aggressive leadership of an up-and-coming general named Napoleon Bonaparte. Before Napoleon took over the French army, it was made up mostly of inexperienced recruits. He reformed it, raised the morale of the troops, and led them to a number of victories using his superior tactics.

Napoleon used his resulting popularity to overthrow the *Directoire* in 1799 and effectively become dictator. Five years later, he crowned himself as the emperor of France.[6]

During most of this time, France was at war, usually against shifting coalitions of other countries that opposed the Revolution. The country's main

Napoleonic Empire at its furthest extent

1805

Napoleon loses battle of Waterloo

1812

1821

British win Battle of Trafalgar

1810

Napoleonic invasion of Russia fails

1815

Napoleon dies in exile

Napoleon around the time of his coronation. Legend has it that Napoleon seized the crown just as Pope Pius VII was about to place it upon Napoleon's head. In reality, the Pope handed the crown to Napoleon, who then crowned himself.

opponent was the British, who handed the French some stinging defeats. The most important was the naval battle of Trafalgar in 1805, which guaranteed that the British would control the seas and kept Napoleon from launching an invasion against them.[7]

On land, however, he remained strong. In 1805, Austria's army joined forces with Russia's, only to be crushed; Austria subsequently agreed to surrender territories to the French. In 1806 Napoleon dissolved the longstanding Holy Roman Empire and added it to his own growing empire. He created a cluster of Germanic states under French rule by consolidating the Rhineland and much of western Germany into the Confederation of the Rhine. Furious, the Prussian king Frederick William III unwisely declared war on France. Within nineteen days, the French had not only defeated the Prussians but also captured Berlin. In early 1807, French troops moved into Eastern Europe to form the Duchy of Warsaw. Later that year, France took Sweden's possessions in northern Germany. Early in 1808, Napoleon invaded Spain and seized Vienna the following year.[8]

French Revolution begins

Napoleon becomes emperor of France

1774

1793

Louis XVI becomes French king

1789

Louis XVI, Marie Antoinette guillotined

1804

By 1810, the French Empire was at its greatest extent. Napoleon controlled France itself, the Swiss Confederation, the Confederation of the Rhine, the Duchy of Warsaw, and the Kingdom of Italy. His allies, ruled by his close relatives, included Spain, the Kingdom of Westphalia, and the Kingdom of Naples. Prussia and Austria also threw their lot in with their former enemies.

In 1812, Napoleon and half a million men invaded Russia. After capturing Moscow, the French army was forced to retreat in the teeth of a brutal Russian winter. Most of his troops perished, and his enemies began to close in. Though he was able to win a few more victories, Napoleon was ultimately pushed back into Paris. On April 6, 1814, he abdicated (gave up) his emperorship. He was exiled to Elba, a small island in the Mediterranean Sea.[9]

The British Royal Navy in the Battle of Trafalgar. The battle pitted the British against the French and Spanish. It was a largely naval battle.

France once again was under the rule of a monarch. The new king was Louis XVIII, the younger brother of the executed Louis XVI.[10] But Napoleon was not ready to give up. Escaping from Elba early in 1815, he moved on to Paris with a hastily drummed-up army and overthrew Louis. Napoleon went on the offensive again. His success was short-lived, and his luck ran out when he was defeated at the Battle of Waterloo on June 18, 1815. He was

1805 — British win Battle of Trafalgar

1810 — Napoleonic Empire at its furthest extent

1812 — Napoleonic invasion of Russia fails

1815 — Napoleon loses battle of Waterloo

1821 — Napoleon dies in exile

Battle of Waterloo. A British soldier recounted the battle's final charge: "[W]e rushed on with fixed bayonets, and that hearty hurrah peculiar to British soldiers."[11]

exiled to Saint Helena, a tiny island in the South Atlantic Ocean, where he died in 1821.

The French Revolution and the Napoleonic Wars represent tumultuous decades in western European history. One brought the ideals of republicanism to the fore. The other made France the most powerful country in western Europe and, just as quickly, brought it to its knees. Both irrevocably changed the map of Europe.

"Let Them Eat Cake"

Marie Antoinette was born as archduchess of Austria in 1755. She left her family at the age of fourteen to join the fifteen-year-old French prince Louis in an arranged marriage. It was not a love match, and Marie Antoinette was homesick and bored by her daily routine.

Her dull life became much more exciting in May 1774, when the French king Louis XV died. Her husband became Louis XVI and Marie Antoinette was now queen of France. She quickly got a reputation as a woman who cared neither for children nor the good of her subjects, but only for gossip and the latest fashions.[12]

Queen Marie Antoinette. Like other monarchs, Marie Antoinette wore the finest fabrics and the latest styles. Stays, a type of corset, cinched her waist, and panniers made her skirt very wide.

Though she became a devoted mother, tempered her extravagant spending, and showed no interest in politics, French citizens held Marie Antoinette partly responsible for their country's economic problems. They were ready to believe any story that cast her in a bad light. Supposedly when someone told her that many people were starving, she replied, "If they have no bread, then let them eat cake."[13] Few historians believe she actually said that.

For several months after the outbreak of the revolution, the royal family was left alone. Then a mob broke into the palace and captured them. More than two years later, Marie Antoinette and her husband were tried and convicted of treason. Still in prison with her children, Marie Antoinette heard the crowds cheer as the king went to the guillotine. Soon thereafter, her eight-year-old son was placed in solitary confinement so that royalists—those who still supported the monarchy—could not liberate the next in line for the throne.

The situation came to a head on October 15, 1793, when a trial convicted Marie Antoinette of treason and sentenced her to die. The next day, a prison guard cut her hair, bound her hands behind her back, and placed her in a cart that wound through the streets of Paris so that crowds could jeer at the humiliated prisoner. After she was publicly beheaded, the executioner held up her head. The crowd, nearly dizzy with excitement, cheered the death of their queen.[14]

Europe in 1815

KINGDOM OF NORWAY AND SWEDEN

SCOTLAND

UNITED KINGDOM OF GREAT BRITAIN AND IRELAND

IRELAND

ENGLAND

London

North Sea

DENMARK

Baltic Sea

•St.Petersburg

•Moscow

RUSSIAN EMPIRE

Amsterdam HANOVER

K. OF THE NETHERLANDS

KINGDOM OF

PRUSSIA

Berlin

•Warsaw

POLAND (to Russia)

Don River

Niemen River

ATLANTIC OCEAN

Paris

Seine R.

Loire River

Rhine R.

SAXONY

BAVARIA

Prague

Danube

River

AUSTRIAN

Vienna

Buda• •Pest

EMPIRE

Dnieper River

Dniester River

Bug River

Pruth River

FRANCE

SWITZ.

Rhone River

VENETIA

LOMBARDY

PARMA

MODENA LUCCA

TUSCANY

PAPAL STATES

Danube

MONTENEGRO

Black Sea

KINGDOM OF SARDINIA

CORSICA (Fr.)

Rome

OTTOMAN

Istanbul•

EMPIRE

PORTUGAL

Tagus River

Madrid

SPAIN

Gibraltar (Br.)

Naples•

KINGDOM OF THE TWO SICILIES

MEDITERRANEAN

SEA

Athens•

MALTA (Br.)

CRETE

CYPRUS

KEY

——— Boundary of the German Confederation

Europe, c. 1815. The end of the Napoleonic Wars left Europe in disarray. European countries sought to redefine their borders and figure out their governments.

Chapter 7

A Century of Isms

After the end of the Napoleonic Wars, western European leaders and citizens alike were tired of war and afraid of the devastation future wars could bring. Britain, Austria, Russia, and Prussia headed up the Congress of Vienna, which met in 1814 and 1815 to formalize a new conservative order. They all agreed that no one country should control most of Europe. They reinstated the French monarchy and surrounded France with strong territories to prevent it from expanding.

It didn't take long for challenges to this new system to arise. In the 1820s, two conflicting groups emerged—nationalists and liberals. According to nationalists, a nation should consist of individuals who shared a common ethnic background, culture, history, and language, and who were governed by one centralized legislative body. Nationalism contradicted the spirit of the Congress of Vienna, which stated that nations were based on monarchies.[1]

Liberalism, on the other hand, stated that individual liberties were more important than national identity. Liberalism was a popular Enlightenment ideal. It was at the core of republican thought. According to liberal thinkers, a relatively weak government should protect the natural rights of the individuals it represented: wealthy property owners. Liberals did not believe in democracy, because they did not believe that the poor should have the same rights as the rich: access to things like freedom of speech and religion, public education, and a virtually unrestricted market economy. Liberals did suggest, however, that government officials answer to the land-owning people, rather than to the monarchy.[2]

Nationalism was the stronger force in the nineteenth century. Nationalists were not intent on overthrowing conservative governments and garnering

The Congress of Vienna, as depicted by Jean-Baptiste Isabey in 1819. Count Metternich (center) presided over the Congress of Vienna. The French foreign minister Charles Maurice de Talleyrand-Perigord and Spain's Marquis of Labrador disrupted the proceedings.

new territory, as Napoleon had done. They took a more academic approach. Many historians who believed in nationalism wrote books on ethnic groups such as the Italians, documenting their history, language, and even dress. Schoolchildren were taught to appreciate their ethnic—and national—heritage. Soon many Europeans thought of themselves in terms of their individual nations.[3]

Nationalists wanted to redraw the European map. However, they could not agree on how to do this.

German nationalists wanted to unite all Germanic peoples under one government. This made for a problematic relationship between Austria and Prussia, two major powers with heavily Germanic populations.[4] Likewise, Italian nationalists wanted all Italian factions on the peninsular "boot" to become one nation.

Liberals, who were largely well-educated and well-off, found that some countries already had liberal-leaning governments. In Great Britain and France, for example, different social classes were represented in a democratic body that balanced out the monarchy. After Napoleon, however, the governments became increasingly conservative. In Great Britain, poorer citizens began demanding Parliamentary change, and radical liberal leaders gained significant followings.[5]

Congress of Vienna seeks lasting peace

1811

1819

1814–1815

Frederick Jahn establishes first gymnasium

Carlsbad Decrees limit political activity

In France, the newly reinstated monarchy was determined to stay in power. King Louis XVIII wanted a constitutional monarchy, but insisted on writing the constitution. The constitution decreed that the French government would have a hereditary monarchy and a legislature. This was an agreeable situation for French liberals, but extreme conservatives—also known as ultraroyalists—could not stomach it. By the early 1820s, the ultraroyalists had convinced Louis that liberals wanted to sabotage his rule. The king and his friends gave more power to aristocrats, and persecuted liberals.[6]

King Louis VIII of France in his ceremonial garb. Louis had several titles in addition to King of France: Count of Provence, Duke of Anjou, and Duke of Vendome.

In the German Confederation, liberals had never been well represented in government. Unlike British or French liberals, German liberals had some nationalistic beliefs. They supported the unification of German-speaking Europe with Austria or Prussia leading the way. The powerful rulers of Prussia and Austria were alarmed by the demands of Germanic liberals. The Austrian prince Klemens von Metternich was particularly keen on squashing liberals' hopes. He feared that unification of the small Germanic states would decrease Austria's power. The ethnic groups populating Germanic territories—such as Hungarians, Poles, Czechs, Slovenes, Italians, and Croats—would gain a voice in a centralized government.

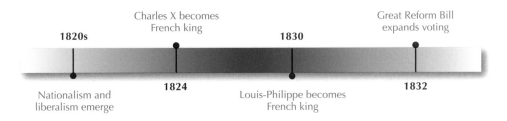

Charles X becomes French king

Great Reform Bill expands voting

1820s

1830

Nationalism and liberalism emerge

1824

Louis-Philippe becomes French king

1832

A liberal movement was afoot among German university students. Prussian king Frederick William III was alarmed at this trend, and took Metternich's advice to draw up the Carlsbad Decrees in 1819. These decrees placed severe limits on student activity, making Prussia less democratic and more monarchical. The Germanic people came under constant scrutiny, and could be severely punished if they spoke out against their rulers.[7]

Beginning in the last half of the 1820s, France and Britain saw their conservative world order begin to crumble. In 1824, Louis died and his brother Charles X ascended the throne.[8] Charles immediately passed laws that favored aristocrats and upset liberals. He thwarted repeated attempts by liberals to dominate the democratically elected cabinet. Things came to a head in July 1830 when downtrodden Parisian labor-

King Charles X, in full coronation dress, as depicted by artist François Gerard. Charles's coronation in 1825 was traditional and elaborate, and was the last of its kind.

ers rioted. Charles sent troops to subdue them. Over 1,800 people died during the subsequent fighting, and the army ended up losing control of Paris. Charles abdicated the throne on August 2 and fled to England.[9]

The Chamber of Deputies installed a constitutional monarchy with Louis-Philippe as king. Unfortunately for the French masses, the new government

1811

Congress of Vienna
seeks lasting peace

1819

Frederick Jahn establishes
first gymnasium

1814–1815

Carlsbad Decrees limit
political activity

Louis-Philippe, the last king of France. During his twenty-one years of exile from France, Louis-Philippe taught geography and mathematics at the college at Richenau in Switzerland under an assumed name.

was only slightly better than the old. Workers' needs were largely ignored, and their revolts were quickly and brutally suppressed.[10]

France's Revolution of 1830 inspired another revolution, this one in Belgium. Belgium had chafed under Dutch rule since 1815, and fighting broke out in August 1830. Belgium declared itself independent in November 1830. Despite the fact that Belgian independence went against the terms imposed by the Congress of Vienna, other European countries recognized the new country.

Charles X becomes French king

1820s

1830

Great Reform Bill expands voting

1824

Louis-Philippe becomes French king

1832

Nationalism and liberalism emerge

House of Commons at Westminster. The House of Commons, House of Lords, and prime minister make up Great Britain's Parliament. Fire destroyed the commons chamber in 1834.

One of these countries was Great Britain, which was undergoing its own, less bloody, revolution. Parliament passed the Great Reform Bill in 1832, giving more English men (but not women) the right to vote. The House of Commons thus became more representative of the British masses.[11]

Whereas earlier European revolutions had been violent and protracted, the revolutions that altered the European map between 1815 and 1830 were largely based on mutual cooperation. But that was soon to change. New, radical ideas of government began to gain popularity just as the Industrial Revolution began to spread through Western Europe. The very nature of monarchies began to change, and major European powers vied for dominance.

Germany and Gymnastics

Every four years, the finest athletes in many nations represent their homelands in the Olympic Games. Television reporters breathlessly update their viewers on the number of medals their countries have won. But nationalism and athletics did not always go hand in hand. Frederick Ludwig Jahn, sometimes referred to as "the father of gymnastics," began this trend. Gymnasts who took pride in their country, he claimed, were "Hardy, Pious, Cheerful, Free."[12]

It all started in 1811 when Jahn established a gymnasium near Berlin. A Prussian, Jahn was mortified when Napoleon took over the Germanic states. To him, anything smacking of foreign influence—including Jews—polluted German purity. Reasoning that Germans who were physically or intellectually weak could not fight such influences, Jahn pushed gymnastics as a way to strengthen young German men. *Turnvereins*, or gymnastic clubs, quickly gained popularity among Germans who shared Jahn's nationalistic beliefs. Gymnasts came to see themselves as fighters for German nationalism.

German gymnast Fabian Hambuechen won a bronze medal in the 2006 Artistic Gymnastics World Championships.

Napoleon's defeat in 1815 kicked off the formation of a number of *turnvereins* across the Germanic states. Gymnasts enjoyed the parallel bars, balance beam, rings, vaulting horse, and horizontal bar—all of which Jahn invented. More than that, however, they defined themselves as Germans and as equals. The gymnasts wore identical uniforms and addressed each other informally. Conservatives soon became leery of the *turnvereins*. Prussia even outlawed gymnastics and imprisoned Jahn for several years.

But the official suppression of gymnastics and nationalism was short-lived. Gymnastics regained popularity in the 1840s, and clubs popped up all over the Germanic states. From the 1840s through 1870, when the German states unified into one nation, gymnastics became increasingly linked to nationalism. Nationalistic fervor remained connected to gymnastics, and then spread to other athletic activities. Today's Olympics are thus the perfect example of how people in the twenty-first century take nationalism for granted.

Prussian influence in Europe, 1862–1871. At this time, Europe was on the verge of imperialism. Much of western Europe was in turmoil as different countries struggled for dominance.

Map labels:

North Sea

Baltic Sea

Memel

HELIGO-LAND (U.K.)

SCHLESWIG

HOLSTEIN

Lübeck

MECKLEN-BURG

Danzig

WEST PRUSSIA

EAST PRUSSIA

Hamburg

OLDEN-BURG

Bremen

RUSSIAN EMPIRE

Amsterdam

HOLLAND

HANOVER

Berlin

Posen

Thorn

Münster

Magdeburg

P R U S S I A

Warsaw

BELGIUM

Brussels

Cologne

HESSE

Weimar

Leipzig

Dresden

Breslau

Lodz

Oppeln

Cracow

Sedan

LUX. Trier

PALATINATE

LORRAINE

Strasbourg

WÜRT-TEMBERG

BAVARIA

Pilsen

Prague

AUSTRIA-HUNGARY

Budweis

Verdun

FRANCE

BADEN

Ulm

Munich

Vienna

ALSACE

Freiburg

SWITZ.

Prussia in 1862

United in 1866–1867, as the North German Confederation

United in 1871

Annexed in 1871, following the Franco-Prussian War

Chapter 8

The Birth of the Nation-State

In the eighteenth and nineteenth centuries, Western Europe experienced wave upon wave of revolution. The nature of revolution changed, from the bloody idealism of the French Revolution to the conservatism of the post-Napoleonic era. By 1830, the tide was changing again. Capitalism bloomed in the guise of the Industrial Revolution.[1]

Not all western Europeans shared in the prosperity. By 1848, several countries were experiencing food shortages, high unemployment, and the squalor of urban life. The first revolution occurred in France. King Louis-Philippe stacked the supposedly liberal government with his supporters. Middle-class French liberals allied with starving and unemployed workers marched through Paris on February 22, 1848. Their numbers and strength grew so rapidly that Louis-Philippe abdicated his throne two days later.[2]

Having achieved their common goal, liberals and workers disagreed about the new government. Liberals planned to write a new constitution. Radical workers demanded that they participate in the constitutional process, but the National Assembly elected on April 23 consisted mostly of moderates and conservatives. After several skirmishes with government troops, radicals were squashed. Louis-Napoleon Bonaparte, Napoleon's nephew, was elected France's president. But Louis-Napoleon, nicknamed the Little Napoleon, was not interested in a republican government. In 1851, he and his supporters staged a bloody coup. The following year, he was crowned Napoleon III, the emperor of France.[3]

The revolution in Paris inspired a core group of Hungarian, German, and Italian nationalists to agitate for cohesive nation-states, much to the ire of the Austrian Empire. In early March, Louis Kossuth incited fellow radicals to march on Vienna, demanding independence for Hungary. When the Austrian army failed to put down the uprising, Metternich fled; the Austrian emperor and his court followed two months later. Encouraged by their successes, Hungarian nationalists tried to bring eastern territories under their rule. At this point, anti-Hungarian forces rallied against the nationalists. In early 1849, Austria squashed the rebellious Hungarians and put them under military rule.

Austria's worries were far from over. Nationalists in northern Italy, which Austria controlled, began agitating for independence. After a brief clash, the Austrian army subdued rebels in Piedmont, the most independent of the Italian states. Radicalism spread to Rome, which was redesigned as the Roman Republic. In March 1849, Piedmont

Napoleon III. In 1836, Napoleon III staged an unsuccessful Napoleonic coup, and was exiled to New York for four years. In 1851 he tried again and was successful. He eventually helped transform Paris into a modern city.

again rose up against Austria and again was defeated. The Roman Republic stood alone. France, fearing that a strong nation could form directly to its south, quickly allied with Austria. Within months, thousands of French troops descended on Rome, and the Roman Republic was history.

Likewise, Germany tried and failed to unify its various states into one nation. In March 1848, rebellions began to spread through several German

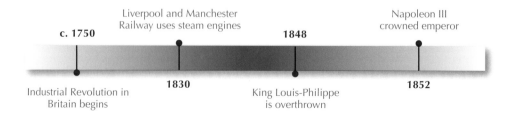

c. 1750

Liverpool and Manchester Railway uses steam engines

1848

Napoleon III crowned emperor

Industrial Revolution in Britain begins

1830

King Louis-Philippe is overthrown

1852

states. German nationalists formed the Frankfurt Parliament, in which they outlined a constitution for a united Germany. But the parliament mainly succeeded in tearing liberals and the working class apart.

In just a few short years, nationalism and liberalism—forces that had been so strong a few decades prior—had been crushed. Conservatism once again reigned. Ironically, it was under a new conservative order that political and geographic change swept through Europe. The Crimean War (1854–

British Grenadier Guards departing from Trafalgar Square in London en route to the Crimea. Great Britain and France were at first reluctant to enter the war.

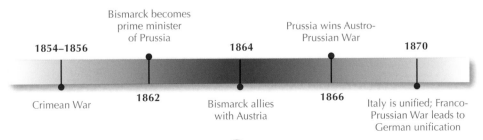

Bismarck becomes prime minister of Prussia
1864

Prussia wins Austro-Prussian War
1870

1854–1856

Crimean War
1862

Bismarck allies with Austria
1866

Italy is unified; Franco-Prussian War leads to German unification

1856)—pitting Russia against Britain, France, and the Turkish Ottoman Empire—marked the beginning of complex conflicts and alliances.[4] Tensions between Austria and Piedmont exploded into an all-out war. Fighting in the Italian provinces of Tuscany, Modena, and Parma added to the melee. Most of northern Italy freed itself from Austrian rule, and much of southern Italy clamored to join their northern compatriots. In 1860, Piedmontese troops captured Austrian-controlled Sicily, then Naples. Within the next decade, Piedmont took over Rome and the northern holdout of Venice. Italian unification was finally completed in 1870.

The unification of Germany rocked Europe both politically and geographically. In 1862, the conservative Otto von Bismarck became Prussia's prime minister. He wanted to create a strong, unified Germany. His vision of a unified Germany included Prussia and the German Confederation, but not Austria. The devious Bismarck formed a formal alliance with Austria in 1864, when the two powers worked together to take over the Danish territories of Schleswig and Holstein. Bismarck then antagonized Austria by mismanaging these new territories, at which point Austria turned to the Germanic states for support. Feigning outrage, Bismarck claimed that Austria had violated their alliance and declared

Otto von Bismarck was also known as Otto Eduard Leopold, Prince of Bismarck, Duke of Lauenburg, Count of Bismarck-Schönhausen. The conservative von Bismarck set the stage for a modern Germany.

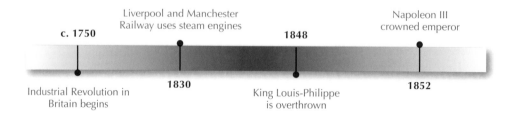

c. 1750

Industrial Revolution in Britain begins

1830

Liverpool and Manchester Railway uses steam engines

1848

King Louis-Philippe is overthrown

Napoleon III crowned emperor

1852

war. The Austro-Prussian War of 1866, also called the Seven Weeks' War, ended with a decisive Prussian victory.[5]

Bismarck was not done. Intent on making the southern Germanic states part of Prussian-controlled Germany, he manipulated European politics. Bismarck watched as Isabella II of Spain was replaced by Prince Leopold, the cousin of Prussian king William I. Threatened by the bond between Spain and Prussia, France calmly expressed its concerns to William, and Leopold stepped down. But France pushed too far, asking William to promise that Leopold would never gain power in Spain. The king refused, and sent Bismarck a telegram detailing this conversation. Bismarck revised the telegram and issued it to the public; the doctored telegram implied that William had disrespected France.[6]

The Battle of Königgrätz (1866) was a turning point in the war between Prussia and Austria. It ended in a Prussian-Italian victory. (The site is in modern-day Czech Republic.)

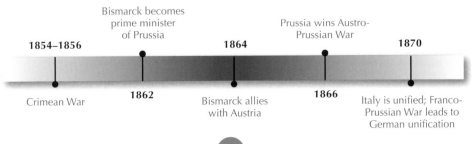

Bismarck becomes prime minister of Prussia

Prussia wins Austro-Prussian War

1854–1856   1864   1870

Crimean War   1862   1866

Bismarck allies with Austria

Italy is unified; Franco-Prussian War leads to German unification

Queen Isabella II of Spain and her eldest daughter, as depicted by artist Franz Xavier Winterhalter in 1852. Isabella was forced into marriage at age sixteen. She eventually bore twelve children, but only four survived to adulthood.

Angered by the supposed insult and intrigued by the prospect of capturing northern Germany, Napoleon III declared war on Prussia in July of 1870. He should have had more foresight. His army was no match for the troops from Prussia and the other Germanic states. The Germans easily quashed the French and captured the ailing Napoleon.[7]

The German Empire was now the centerpiece of Europe, geographically, politically, and economically. It began looking outward. So did the other Western European countries. By this time, revolutions had given way to nation building, and nation-states became the rule rather than the exception. As nations grew stronger, they became increasingly interested in expanding their influence. Many turned to imperialism, and scuffles over borders eventually exploded into World War I.

A Revolution of a Different Kind

The Industrial Revolution changed the character of the European map. It began in England shortly after the mid-1700s as inventors came up with machines that made it much easier to produce textile goods. With these inventions, work once done by hand could now be accomplished in less time and at a lower cost. Textile mills transformed raw cotton and wool into inexpensive fabrics.

By the early nineteenth century, increasingly large factories were filled with machines that made more consumer goods available to the public. It did not take long for people to begin clamoring for what had been luxuries only a few years before—soap, watches, and glassware, just to name a few—that now had become available to them. People of modest means copied the fancier fashions worn by the wealthy classes.[8]

Before long, the Industrial Revolution spread throughout much of Europe. Many Europeans moved from the countryside to cities. Large numbers of young women and men left the farms where they grew up to experience the bustle of city life and the economic freedom of wage-earning.

To get raw materials to factories and finished goods to consumers in an inexpensive and efficient manner, turnpikes, canals, and railroads were built. Turnpikes—roads that charged tolls to keep them in good condition—were a vast improvement over the old, rutted roads that were poorly maintained. Entrepreneurs also began building canals, which created shortcuts between rivers and lakes and linked major manufacturing centers.

The most significant improvement in transportation came with the building of the railroads. At the beginning of the nineteenth century, people and goods began riding on horse-drawn trains. In the late 1820s, steam engines began taking over; England's Liverpool and Manchester Railway was the first company to use steam engines when it opened operations on 31 miles of track in 1830.[9] The growth was rapid. In 1836, there were 1,000 miles of track in England; sixteen years later, there were more than 7,000 miles.[10]

A spinning jenny. A mechanized version of the manual spinning wheel, the spinning jenny spun fibers into thread. It was invented in the early 1760s and became widespread in factories soon thereafter.

Europe, c. 1914. In the years leading up to World War I, several European countries developed into modern superpowers. Struggles for power brought about new enemies and new alliances.

Chapter 9

Imperialism and the Great War

Imperialism was not a new practice, as European countries had colonized other lands for centuries. After years of political strife, the only European power with significant overseas territories was Great Britain. In the 1870s, imperialism was revived and became a way of life for Western Europeans. Loyal, patriotic citizens felt it only right to exploit other lands for their own benefit. They believed they were physically, intellectually, and morally superior to non-Europeans. In fact, they often felt that they were doing smaller countries a favor by taking them over.

European nations spread, octopus-like, over roughly one-fifth of the earth's landmass, eventually controlling about one-tenth of the world's population.[1] They often put the native inhabitants to work building railroads, excavating mines, and planting cash crops. As a result, they made huge profits, and also garnered special trading privileges with the weaker governments.

Africa became the main focus. Within a short time, Europeans controlled all of northern Africa, and most of the rest of the continent. They came to rely on Africa's raw materials, such as ivory, rubber, and diamonds.[2]

In Asia, the British and the French became the dominant forces of imperialism. The British ruled India and Burma. The French laid claim to Cambodia, Laos, and Vietnam. The Dutch controlled the East Indies. Everyone, it seemed, had a part of China.[3]

The scramble for colonies sometimes threatened to break out into open conflict. That wasn't the only source of disagreement as the nineteenth century began to move toward its close. As Europe's new nation-states strove to become more powerful, they inevitably stepped on each other's toes. This caused tensions and resulted in alliances among different nations.

France remained angry after being defeated in the Franco-Prussian War.[4] Bismarck worried that France would ally itself with Austria or Russia against Germany. He was also concerned that Russia and Austria would go to war against each other and Germany would get sucked into the conflict. In 1879, Bismarck secretly forged the Dual Alliance with Austria. Both countries pledged to help each other if Russia attacked one of them, and to remain

The Battle of Mars-la-Tour, in August 1870, during the Franco-Prussian War. A British war correspondent said about one of the battles: "[I]t was evident that something very like a decisive engagement would take place, and that either the French or the German army would be badly beaten before many hours were over."[5]

Italy, Germany, and Austria
forge Triple Alliance

Germany starts arms
race at sea

1879   **1894**   **1904**

1882   **1898**

Germany and Austria
forge Dual Alliance

Franco-Russian
Alliance formed

Great Britain and France
in Entente Cordiale

neutral if another country waged war against either one. The Dual Alliance became the Triple Alliance three years later when Italy joined. The three countries mistrusted France and Russia.[6]

The delicate balance of power began changing in 1890, when the ambitious young William II, Germany's new ruler, fired Bismarck. Without Bismarck's cunning, William could not prevent France from forming an alliance with Russia in 1894.

To add salt to Germany's wounds, Great Britain became disenchanted with William. In 1898, William committed his country to an ambitious program of naval construction so that Germany could compete with the British on the high seas. That led to a very expensive arms race, and served primarily to alarm the British and push them toward an agreement known as the Entente Cordiale (awn-TAUNT kawr-DYAL, which means "friendly understanding") with their longtime enemy, France, in 1904. Three years later, Russia joined them in the Triple Entente.[7]

The two sides kept a close watch on each other. In 1908, Austria-Hungary seized Bosnia, a small country in Eastern Europe. Serbia, which shared boundaries with both Bosnia and Austria-Hungary, was angry. It wanted Bosnia for itself. Russia threw its support behind the Serbs, which heightened tensions even more between the two alliances.

Tensions tipped toward full-scale war on June 28, 1914. A Serbian nationalist shot and killed the Austrian archduke Franz Ferdinand and his wife. Backed by Germany, Austria-Hungary declared war on Serbia a month later. This declaration had a domino effect. In support of Serbia, Russia announced that it was mobilizing. That means they moved troops and supplies into position to launch an attack. In response, Germany declared war on Russia on August 1. Two days later, Germany declared war on France. German troops invaded France through Belgium, violating Belgium's neutrality. Great Britain, angered by this violation, entered the war against the Triple Alliance on August 4.[8]

1907	World War I begins	1917	Fighting ends with armistice	1919
Great Britain, France, and Russia form Triple Entente	1914	United States enters World War I	1918	War ends with Treaty of Versailles

The Great War, as it was called at the time, focused on two areas: the Eastern Front and the Western Front. The Eastern Front ran roughly along the Russian border, while the Western Front cut through northern France from the sea to the Swiss border.

Both sides expected a short war. They were wrong. Neither side could win a decisive victory. New military technologies ultimately resulted in the deaths of millions of men. The Triple Entente gained a small advantage in 1915 when Italy switched sides, though it didn't have a major impact. The war remained stalemated through 1916 and most of 1917. The Russian Revolution that November overthrew the country's czar, or ruler. The country's new communist government quickly ended hostilities with Germany, which shifted the troops fighting there to the Western Front.

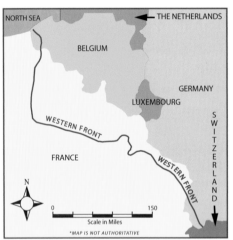

On the Western Front, the French and British armies fought the Germans. On the Eastern Front, Russian troops faced the combined armies of Germany and Austria-Hungary. Millions of men faced each other in lines of trenches only a few hundred yards apart. Although the lines did not remain fixed throughout the war, very little territory changed hands in three years of fighting.

New and reconstituted nations

FINLAND

NORWAY

SWEDEN

ESTONIA

North Sea

DENMARK

LATVIA

Danzig (Free City)

LITHUANIA

GREAT BRITAIN

GER.

RUSSIA

NETH.

GERMANY

POLAND

BELG.

LUX.

CZECHOSLOVAKIA

FRANCE

SWITZ.

AUSTRIA

HUNGARY

ROMANIA

YUGOSLAVIA

SPAIN

Corsica (Fr.)

ITALY

BULGARIA

Mallorca (Sp.)

Sardinia (It.)

ALBANIA

Mediterranean Sea

GREECE

ALGERIA (Fr.)

TUNISIA (Fr.)

Sicily

Crete

Europe, c. 1918. At the end of World War I, the Treaty of Versailles carved out several new nations. Some were better off, but others—most importantly, Germany—suffered greatly.

World War I begins

1907

1917

Fighting ends with armistice

1919

1914

United States enters World War I

1918

War ends with Treaty of Versailles

Great Britain, France, and Russia form Triple Entente

The palace at Versailles. For many centuries, Versailles played an important role in government operations. Several treaties were signed there, including the ones that ended the American Revolution and World War I.

A German offensive the following spring against the exhausted French and British defenders might well have succeeded in ending the war. By then, American troops had become an important factor. The United States had actually declared war on Germany in April 1917, but it required more than a year to raise an army, train it, transport it across the Atlantic, and enter the fighting.

Now the fresh American troops helped the French and British push back the Germans. Its resources and morale exhausted, Germany signed an armistice on November 11, 1918, ending the fighting.

The war officially ended in June 1919 with the Treaty of Versailles (vair-SY). This agreement mapped out the future of the Europe, as new nations such as Czechoslovakia, Hungary, Austria, Yugoslavia, Finland, Estonia, Latvia, and Lithuania emerged from the old Russian, German, and Austro-Hungarian Empires. In addition, Germany had to relinquish the territory it had taken from France, Belgium, Denmark, and Poland.[9]

Unfortunately, what many people hoped would be the "war to end all wars" did not live up to its name. It set the stage for an even more destructive and bloody conflict that would get under way almost exactly two decades after the signing of the Treaty of Versailles.

Barbed Wire and Big Berthas

World War I was a grueling, bloody conflict. It was made all the more gruesome as old military strategies met new technology. Along the Western Front, millions of German troops faced an equal number of French and British soldiers in a complex system of trenches that paralleled each other. Barbed wire and land mines fortified the trenches. Between the two lines of trenches was a "no-man's-land."[10]

For the most part, soldiers hunkered down in the trenches, peering out only to attack the enemy with new rapid-fire rifles or explosives. Soldiers lived and died in these muddy trenches. They ate and slept among rats, lice, and corpses of their fallen compatriots. Many were killed or wounded from head wounds caused by flying shrapnel—razor-sharp pieces of steel produced by exploding artillery shells.

Sometimes they would launch attacks that would begin with long artillery bombardments. In the beginning, some of these bombardments included the legendary Big Bertha, a German cannon that flung a shell weighing nearly a ton over distances of up to ten miles.[11] When the big guns fell silent, the men would scramble out of their trenches and head for the enemy. Many would be cut down far short of their goal by machine guns, which probably accounted for more battlefield deaths than any other weapon.

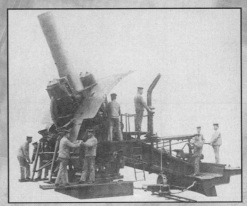

Big Bertha, a type of howitzer capable of destroying enemy forts. At the beginning of World War I, there were only six Big Berthas in existence.

There were still more forms of new weaponry. Though they often broke down, tanks lumbered across decimated land, deflecting bullets and destroying everything in their path. Poisonous chemicals—including mustard gas, nerve gas, and chlorine—were released, and many soldiers suffered blindness or neurological damage as a result.[12] The relatively new airplane made it possible to fight in the air, and U-boats, or submarines, snuck up on enemy ships and sent them to the bottom with a spread of torpedoes.

Modern warfare had begun.

EUROPE
German Agressions,
1936 - 1939

German expansion in the 1930s. In the years prior to World War II, Germany built up its empire under Adolf Hitler. It did so mostly through treachery and strong-arm tactics. Meanwhile, the U.S.S.R., or the Union of Soviet Socialist Republics, was formed. It was also known as the Soviet Union.

Chapter 10

World War II and the Cold War

When the Great Depression began sweeping through Europe in 1929, many people endured unemployment, homelessness, or other forms of deprivation. Germans felt the Depression most keenly because they suffered from massive inflation and were still making huge payments to the victors of World War I. To make matters worse, the government was unstable. Germans wanted a powerful leader, and they found one in Adolf Hitler.

Hitler was ambitious, charismatic, and a powerful orator. He cloaked his beliefs in an extreme form of nationalism and packaged his ideas in a political party: the National Socialist German Worker's Party, also known as the Nazi Party.[1]

After becoming dictator of Germany in 1933, Hitler rebuilt the German army and spread his prejudices throughout the country. He sent the Gestapo, or the secret police, to imprison or murder those who opposed him. Hitler's biggest ambition, though, was not merely to fix the economic problems that Germans faced, but to "purify" and expand the German Empire. This ambition for purification led to the establishment of concentration camps, which eventually resulted in the deaths of millions of people in the Holocaust.[2]

His program of expansion began in 1936 when he sent troops into the Rhineland, a German region that lay next to the French border. Even though this action directly contradicted the Treaty of Versailles, neither Britain nor France did anything. In March 1938, he annexed Austria. In September, he persuaded Britain and France to allow Germany to take over the Sudetenland, a German-speaking region in Czechoslovakia. German troops occupied the rest of Czechoslovakia the following March.

Two months later, he and Italian dictator Benito Mussolini signed a military alliance. Germany invaded Poland on September 1, 1939, which marked the beginning of World War II. Two days later, Britain and France declared war on Germany. They couldn't stop Hitler's rapid conquest of Poland. The following spring, Germany overran nearly all of Western Europe. France, which had resisted Germany for more than four years in World War I, fell to onrushing German troops in less than two months.

Great Britain became Hitler's only remaining major opponent, as the United States remained neutral. The Germans launched a bombing campaign against the British that began in fall 1940 and lasted through the following summer. Under the inspired leadership of Winston Churchill, Great Britain refused to give in.

Hitler invaded the Soviet Union (founded in 1922, it consisted of Russia and fourteen other republics) in

Adolf Hitler, the fascist dictator who led Germany into World War II. One of the most brutal dictators in world history, he committed suicide at the close of the war.

June 1941. German troops and tanks made great inroads at first, but the harsh winter stopped them in their tracks, freezing many soldiers to death.[3]

The war changed on December 7, 1941, when the Japanese—who were allied with Germany and Italy—attacked the U.S. naval base at Pearl Harbor,

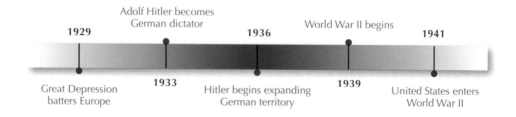

Adolf Hitler becomes
German dictator

1929

1936

World War II begins

1941

Great Depression
batters Europe

1933

Hitler begins expanding
German territory

1939

United States enters
World War II

Benito Mussolini. American school-children made fun of the Italian dictator with a schoolyard chant: "A tisket, a tasket, Hitler in a basket, eenie meenie Mussolini, hit him with a hatchet."

Hawaii. The United States became involved in the war, both in Europe and in the Pacific Ocean, as allies with the British and the Soviets. Slowly the tide of war turned. Italy surrendered in 1943. British, Canadian, and American troops invaded France in June 1944 and pushed toward Germany. At the same time, the Soviets were applying pressure from the east. Utterly defeated, Hitler committed suicide the following April, and Germany surrendered a few days later. The war officially ended in August with Japan's surrender.

World War II was almost immediately followed by a war of a different character: the Cold War. Rooted in distrust between the United States and the Soviet Union, the conflict greatly affected Western Europe. During World War II, the United States and the Soviet Union were united in their hatred of Nazi Germany. But the two sides had long seen each other as fundamentally different. The United States was a democracy, whereas the Soviet Union was a communist nation.

Tensions surfaced as soon as the war was over. Germany was divided into four zones of occupation: American, British, French, and Soviet. It

North Atlantic Treaty Organization (NATO) forms

1945

1955

East Germans fortify border

1989

World War II ends

1949

Warsaw Pact forms

1961

Cold War officially over

quickly became apparent that the Soviets and the three Western powers couldn't agree on the best way to govern Germany as a whole.

Germany was just one problem area. In 1947 the American government instituted the policy of containment. Western democracies would "contain" communism within its current borders and keep it from spreading.[4] One key

The Yalta Conference of 1945. From left to right are the "Big Three": Great Britain's Winston Churchill, U.S. President Franklin D. Roosevelt, and the Soviet leader Joseph Stalin. The Yalta Conference was the most significant of three conferences held near the end of the war.

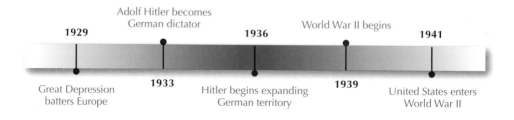

Adolf Hitler becomes German dictator

1929

1936

World War II begins

1941

Great Depression batters Europe

1933

Hitler begins expanding German territory

1939

United States enters World War II

element of the policy was the Marshall Plan, under which the United States donated billions of dollars to western European governments to rebuild their economies.[5] The alliance between the United States and Western Europe became official in 1949 with the formation of the North Atlantic Treaty Organization (NATO).[6] The United States and Canada joined ten Western European countries in an alliance to deter Soviet aggression. Six years later, the Soviets responded with the Warsaw Pact, heading a group that included seven other countries in Eastern Europe with communist governments.

The attack on Pearl Harbor. Japanese warcraft destroyed five American battleships, three destroyers, a minelayer, and a target ship. It also damaged many other ships and aircraft. As a result, the United States entered World War II.

North Atlantic Treaty Organization (NATO) forms

East Germans fortify border

1945   1955   1989

World War II ends   1949   Warsaw Pact forms   1961   Cold War officially over

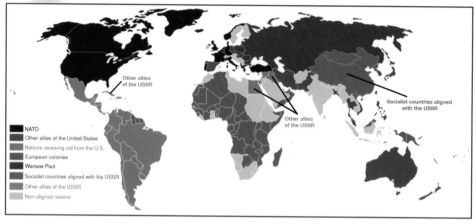

The Cold War, 1959. During the early years of the Cold War, the Americans and Soviets built up a distrust that lasted for several decades. Since then, the United States and Russia have worked to build a productive relationship.

After peaking in the 1950s and early 1960s, Cold War tensions began to subside. Over the course of most of the 1970s, the two sides frequently engaged in diplomatic talks. But in the late 1970s and into the 1980s, the Cold War experienced another spike in activity. Americans and Soviets once again feared that the other would launch an all-out war. In the early 1980s, the Americans installed missiles in Western Europe that were aimed at Eastern Europe. The Soviets continued their high expenditures on their military.

The Soviet economy was crumbling, so it couldn't maintain such a high level of military spending. In December 1989, the leaders of the United States and the Soviet Union declared an end to the Cold War.[7] Two years later, the Soviet Union broke up. Since then, all of Europe has experienced a gradual change. There is no longer a hard line dividing Eastern and Western Europe. The two sides are working to unite through the European Union.

The Holocaust

The Holocaust is a term that conjures up horrifying images from the World War II era. Nazi officers rounding up men, women, and children and forcing them into ghettos; starving prisoners working in concentration camps; bodies lying in heaps after being gassed.

Adolf Hitler wanted to create a German Empire populated only by people of the "Aryan race." In his view, Aryans were people of Northern European descent. He believed they were better than any other group of people. Hitler especially looked down on Jews, so he wanted to be sure that there was hardly any contact between Jews and Aryans.

At first, the Nazi regime implemented laws designed to drive Jews from Germany. Jewish-owned stores were boycotted and vandalized, Jews could no longer be bankers or hold other jobs in finance, synagogues (Jewish places of worship) were trashed. Then the Nazis upped the ante. They shipped Polish and Western European Jews to tightly packed ghettos, where nobody was allowed to leave. Many died there from malnutrition and disease.

Soon the Holocaust became even more deadly. The Nazis established dozens of concentration camps in Germany and Eastern Europe where Jews were underfed, underdressed, and forced to work long hours at brutal jobs. If they did not perish from starvation, disease, or overwork, they were murdered in gas chambers. Their bodies were burned in large ovens called crematoria. Under Hitler's rule, Nazis persecuted and exterminated roughly six million, or two-thirds, of Europe's Jews. Other "undesirables"—also slated for extermination—included Roma (Gypsies), homosexuals, and people with mental or physical handicaps.

Children of the Holocaust

These killings finally came to an end when Allied forces made their way across Germany in 1945. They liberated many emaciated and terrorized prisoners who had somehow managed to stay alive.

Not surprisingly, a number of Holocaust survivors left their homelands for Israel, which was established in 1948 as a Jewish state. Thousands of others fled to live with relatives in the United States or in other nations.[8]

The European Union in 2001

- European Union
- Economic and Monetary Union
- EFTA
- Candidate Countries

0   100   500 km

ICELAND

ATLANTIC OCEAN

Norwegian Sea

NORWAY

SWEDEN

FINLAND

North Sea

ESTONIA

LATVIA

IRELAND

DENMARK

Baltic Sea

LITHUANIA

UNITED KINGDOM

NETHERLANDS

POLAND

GERMANY

BELGIUM

LUXEMBOURG

CZECH REPUBLIC

SLOVAKIA

FRANCE

LIECHTENSTEIN
SWITZERLAND

AUSTRIA

HUNGARY

ROMANIA

SLOVENIA

Black Sea

ITALY

BULGARIA

PORTUGAL

SPAIN

TURKEY

GREECE

MEDITERRANEAN SEA

MALTA

CYPRUS

The European Union (EU) and European Free Trade Area (EFTA) in 2001. At the end of the Cold War, Europeans warmed to the idea of a unified Europe. Many countries jumped at the chance to join the European Union, which has continued to grow.

Chapter 11

From Iron Curtain to European Union

The Iron Curtain, the symbolic dividing line between Eastern and Western Europe, came crashing down at the end of World War II.[1] But even before the war ended, Europeans were migrating from country to city, and from one nation to another. The end of the war displaced millions of people, and some European borders were redrawn, usually to the detriment of Germany. Millions of Germans were driven from their homes in territory that now belonged to Poland, Czechoslovakia, and other countries. Enormous numbers of other Europeans willingly left their homes, seeking freedom from ethnic persecution or better economic opportunities.

Many Europeans returned to Europe after living in overseas colonies. France especially experienced massive decolonization as French citizens flocked back from places like Algeria. The British Empire was downsized, causing mass migration to Great Britain. The movement toward Indonesian independence forced the Dutch to return to their homeland. Similarly, Belgians left the Belgian Congo, and Portuguese left Mozambique and Angola.

But it was not just European colonials returning to their birthplaces. Native inhabitants of various colonies also emigrated. Lifelong residents of the Caribbean, Africa, and India traveled to Great Britain, while natives of Africa, Indochina, and some Arab nations moved to France.[2]

During these mass migrations, many Europeans became interested in formally unifying the continent. Eastern Europe functioned largely under Soviet rule. The United States, embroiled in the Cold War against the Soviet Union, wanted to strengthen Western Europe. Western Europeans did not need much urging, as they saw themselves as economically and politically weak com-

pared to the Soviets. They began working together with the Marshall Plan and NATO.

France, West Germany, Italy, Belgium, the Netherlands, and Luxembourg kicked off this new era of cooperation in 1951 when they established the European Coal and Steel Community (ECSC). Highly productive and beneficial to its members, the ESCS encouraged unity among Western Europeans.[3]

The road to further unity, however, was rough. Great Britain and France embarrassed themselves in 1956 when they fought Egypt regarding ownership of the Suez Canal. They were forced to back down. The Suez crisis convinced many people that Western Europeans needed to present a united front if they wished to stand up to the two superpowers, the United States and the Soviet Union.

In 1957, the six ECSC countries expanded their economic vision for Western Europe. They signed the Treaty of Rome, which established the European Economic Community (EEC).[4] Also called the Common Market, the EEC was wildly successful in its plan to establish a system of give-and-take across European borders. Instead of tariffs and taxes on

An aerial view of the Suez Canal. Located in Egypt, the Suez Canal is 101 miles long and allows boats to transport goods between Africa and Asia. In 1956, countries fought over its ownership.

| 1947 | European Coal and Steel Community (ECSC) formed | 1956 | European Economic Community (EEC) founded | 1960 |

Marshall Plan helps Western Europe
1951
Suez Canal crisis
1957
European Free Trade Area (EFTA) established

imports and exports, they hoped there would be a system of free trade. True to their word, the six founders of the EEC eliminated tariffs among themselves by 1968. They also hoped that citizens of one country would be able to work easily in another one, and all workers would enjoy the same standard of pay and social services such as health care.

The early progress of the EEC inspired similar organizations. Three years after the EEC was established, the European Free Trade Area (EFTA) came about.[5] It consisted of Great Britain, Denmark, Norway, Sweden, Switzerland, Austria, and Portugal. Within two years, however, the British set their

The Treaty of Rome was signed by France, West Germany, Italy, and Benelux (Belgium, the Netherlands, and Luxembourg) on March 25, 1957. The treaty established the European Economic Community (EEC), and would be in effect beginning January 1958.

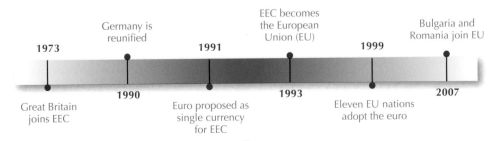

1973 — Great Britain joins EEC
1990
Germany is reunified — 1991
Euro proposed as single currency for EEC
1993
EEC becomes the European Union (EU)
1999
Eleven EU nations adopt the euro
Bulgaria and Romania join EU — 2007

91

sights on joining the EEC. During the next decade, France turned the British away three times, claiming that Great Britain's allegiance to the United States would hurt the EEC. It was not until 1973 that Great Britain, along with Ireland and Denmark, officially joined the EEC.

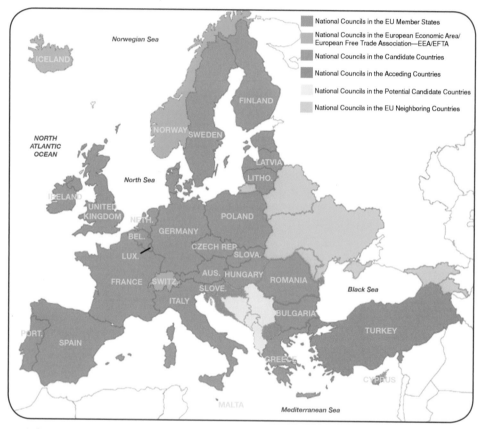

By February 2007, many more European countries had joined the EU. Several others were candidates for membership.

Problems arose in the late 1970s and early 1980s. Members of the EEC began fighting among themselves. Norway and Sweden refused to add their healthy economies to the organization.

The EEC rallied and set the tone for modern Europe. In the late 1980s, it pledged that its members would be freed from trade restrictions within four years. The 1991 Treaty of Maastricht facilitated this process. It set the stage for a strong central European bank and a single European currency, the euro.[6]

Euro coins and bank notes. By 2007, at least twelve countries in the European Union were using the Euro. Great Britain was one of the more prominent holdouts, as it was still using pounds and pence.

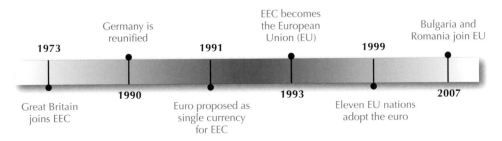

Germany is reunified
1991
EEC becomes the European Union (EU)
1999
Bulgaria and Romania join EU

1973

1990
Euro proposed as single currency for EEC

1993

Eleven EU nations adopt the euro

2007

Great Britain joins EEC

José Manuel Barroso, President of the European Commission, which is the executive branch of the European Union. The president is elected by the council of national governments, then must be approved by the European Parliament. This multinational group of representatives meets in Strasbourg, France, and in Brussels, Belgium.

After overcoming some obstacles, the treaty was approved in 1993. At this point, the EEC transformed into the European Union (EU), and again began adding new members. A dramatic enlargement occurred in 2004 when ten eastern European countries joined the organization. Bulgaria and Romania joined the EU on January 1, 2007, bringing the total number of member nations to twenty-seven. A number of others were waiting in the wings for acceptance, some of them not even in Europe proper.

The euro experienced a similar pattern of acceptance. While the idea was presented to Europe in 1993, it was not until 1999 that it was introduced into the economies of eleven nations. There remained some significant holdouts in 2007, including Great Britain, Sweden, and Denmark.[7]

The euro isn't the only issue. A proposed European Union constitution divided the member nations, causing much infighting over the extent of free trade and other issues. As a result, the future of unification remains to be seen.

German Reunification

Between 1939 and 1945, Germany suffered about 10 million military and civilian casualties. Many of its cities were little more than piles of rubble. Yet Germans were determined to recover, and they set their sights on reunification.

This turned out to be quite a challenge. Nearly powerless, Germany was divided into four occupation zones, controlled by the United States, Great Britain, France, and the Soviet Union. From the start, the Soviets butted heads with the three western powers. They even tried to deny access to Berlin in June 1948. Although the city lay deep within their territory, it had also been divided among the four powers. This led to the Berlin Airlift, which lasted almost a year.[8] Hundreds of airplanes flying almost continuously delivered more than two million tons of supplies to the city before the Soviets called off the blockade in May 1949. Later that year, the three Western zones of occupation became the Federal Republic of Germany, or West Germany. The Soviet Union, in turn, created the German Democratic Republic, or East Germany, from its zone of occupation a few months later.

West Germany quickly began to show significant economic growth and later became an important member of NATO and the EEC. East Germany also fared well, at least in comparison to other countries under Soviet control. However, many East Germans craved the democratic freedoms they saw in West Germany. Many emigrated there. This migration came to almost a complete halt in 1961 when the East German government constructed a heavily fortified border. The infamous Berlin Wall was part of this border. Many people who tried to leave East Germany were shot and killed. The barriers remained in place for nearly thirty years.

East Germany loosened the border restrictions late in 1989. Jubilant Germans attacked the Berlin Wall with pick-axes, spray cans, and their bare hands.[9] The country became reunified within a year.

Today, Germany is made up of sixteen states and 439 districts. Each of these states has a capital city, but all answer to the national capital of Berlin. With more than 80 million inhabitants, it is the most populous country in Western Europe.

The Fall of the Berlin Wall in 1989

750 BCE	Estruscans rule the Romans.
509 BCE	Rome overthrows Etruscan monarchy and becomes a republic.
343–146 BCE	Rome expands as a republic during a series of conflicts, most notably the Punic Wars.
60 BCE	Pompey the Great, Julius Caesar, and Marcus Crassus form the First Triumvirate.
44 BCE	Julius Caesar is assassinated in the Roman Senate.
27 BCE	Augustus Caesar becomes the first Roman emperor.
79 CE	Mt. Vesuvius erupts, burying two cities under a thick layer of volcanic ash.
117	Emperor Trajan dies; the Roman Empire reaches its furthest territorial extent.
284	Emperor Diocletian divides the Roman Empire into western and eastern halves.
330	Emperor Constantine establishes eastern capital at Constantinople.
410	The Visigoths, a tribe of barbarians, sack Rome.
476	The Western Roman Empire falls as Odoacer deposes Romulus Augustus, the final emperor.
732	Charles Martel defeats Islamic army at the Battle of Tours.
800	Pope Leo III crowns Charlemagne as "Emperor of the Romans."
843	Charlemagne's grandsons divide their father's territories among themselves.
962	Pope John XII crowns Otto I as emperor to mark the beginning of the Holy Roman Empire.
c. 1000	The High Middle Ages begin.
1066	Norman French under William the Conqueror defeat English at the Battle of Hastings.
1087	Construction begins on St. Paul's Cathedral.
1150	The University of Paris is established.
1215	English barons force King John I to sign the Magna Carta.
c. 1300	The Late Middle Ages begin.
1315	The Great Famine begins; it results in the starvation of millions of people.
1337–1453	France and England fight the Hundred Years' War over control of the French throne.
1347	The Black Death begins and soon claims up to one-third of the population of Western Europe.
1453	Muslim armies capture Constantinople, which marks the end of the Eastern Roman Empire.
1494	Italian Wars begin as France invades northern Italy.
1517	German monk Martin Luther begins the Protestant Reformation.

1543	Astronomer Nicolaus Copernicus publishes the highly controversial *On the Revolutions of the Heavenly Spheres*.
1559	The Italian Wars end.
1648	The Dutch receive their independence from Spain.
1652	The first Anglo-Dutch War begins.
1654	The first Anglo-Dutch War ends.
1660	Charles II becomes king of England.
1664	The second Anglo-Dutch War begins.
1666	The Great Fire of London destroys most of the city's homes and businesses.
1667	The second Anglo-Dutch War ends.
1687	Isaac Newton publishes his book *Principia*, which describes the theory of gravity.
1739	England and Spain fight the War of Jenkins' Ear.
1740	The War of the Austrian Succession begins and soon involves much of Western Europe.
1748	The War of the Austrian Succession ends with little change in borders.
c. 1750	The Enlightenment reaches its peak; the Industrial Revolution in Britain begins with the invention of several machines that speed up textile production.
1756	The Seven Years' War begins.
1763	The Seven Years' War ends; France loses nearly all of its New World possessions.
1774	Louis XVI becomes French king, and Marie Antoinette becomes queen.
1789	The French Revolution begins with the storming of the Bastille.
1793	Louis XVI and Marie Antoinette are guillotined.
1804	Napoleon is proclaimed as emperor of France.
1805	The British Navy defeats the French fleet at the Battle of Trafalgar.
1806	The Holy Roman Empire is dissolved and becomes part of the Napoleonic Empire.
1810	The Napoleonic Empire reaches its furthest extent.
1811	Frederick Ludwig Jahn establishes a gymnasium near Berlin.
1812	Napoleon invades Russia; he captures Moscow but is forced to retreat and loses most of his army.
1814–1815	Great Britain, Russia, Prussia, and Austria convene the Congress of Vienna, which seeks to establish a permanent peace in Europe.
1815	Napoleon is defeated at the Battle of Waterloo and is exiled to St. Helena.

1819	The Carlsbad Decrees place severe limits on German students' political activity.
1820s	Nationalism and liberalism begin to emerge in Western Europe.
1821	Napoleon dies in exile at St. Helena.
1824	Charles X becomes the king of France.
1830	Louis-Philippe becomes French king after the July Revolution; Belgium becomes independent; the Liverpool and Manchester Railway becomes the first company to use steam engines.
1832	The Great Reform Bill in Britain provides voting rights for many more English men.
1848	King Louis-Philippe is overthrown.
1852	Louis-Napoleon Bonaparte, or "Little Napoleon," is crowned Napoleon III, the emperor of France.
1854–1856	The Crimean War pits Russia against France, Britain, and the Ottoman Empire.
1862	Otto von Bismarck becomes the prime minister of Prussia and begins working toward German unification.
1864	Bismarck establishes a formal alliance with Austria.
1866	Bismarck's maneuvering leads to the Austro-Prussian War, which ends in a Prussian victory.
1870	Napoleon III begins the Franco-Prussian War, which ends early the following year with a decisive Prussian victory and German unification.
1879	Germany and Austria form the Dual Alliance.
1882	Italy joins Germany and Austria to establish the Triple Alliance.
1894	Fearing Germany, France, and Russia form the Franco-Russian Alliance.
1898	Germany begins a very expensive arms race at sea, challenging British naval superiority.
1904	Great Britain and France establish the Entente Cordiale.
1907	Great Britain, France, and Russia form the Triple Entente.
1914	World War I begins with the Triple Alliance in conflict with the Triple Entente.
1917	The United States enters World War I; the Russian Revolution overthrows the czar and installs a communist government.
1918	The fighting in World War I ends as the Germans agree to an armistice.

Timeline

1919	The Treaty of Versailles officially ends World War I; it cripples Germany economically.
1929	The Great Depression adversely affects Western Europe.
1933	Adolf Hitler becomes the dictator of Germany.
1936	Hitler begins his program of expansion, violating the terms of the Treaty of Versailles.
1939	The Germany Army invades Poland, and World War II begins.
1941	Hitler invades Russia; the United States enters World War II after being attacked by Japan.
1945	World War II ends in Europe in May with the German surrender; Japan surrenders in August.
1947	The United States provides billions of dollars under the Marshall Plan to help Western Europe rebuild.
1949	The North Atlantic Treaty Organization (NATO) is formed among the United States, Canada, and ten Western European countries.
1951	France, West Germany, Italy, Belgium, the Netherlands, and Luxembourg form the European Coal and Steel Community (ECSC).
1955	The Soviet Union and seven other countries form the Warsaw Pact.
1956	Great Britain and France lose face in the Suez Canal crisis.
1957	The six ECSC countries found the European Economic Community (EEC).
1960	Great Britain, Denmark, Norway, Sweden, Switzerland, Austria, and Portugal establish the European Free Trade Area (EFTA).
1961	The East Germans fortify the border with West Germany, including setting up the Berlin Wall.
1973	Great Britain joins the European Economic Community.
1989	The United States and the Soviet Union declare that the Cold War is officially over; East Germany relaxes border restrictions.
1990	Germany is reunified, with its capital in Berlin.
1991	The Treaty of Maastricht proposes a single currency for all of Europe, the euro.
1993	The European Economic Community becomes the European Union (EU).
1999	The euro becomes the common currency in eleven European Union nations.
2007	Bulgaria and Romania join the European Union.

Chapter Notes

Chapter 1. The Great Fire of London

1. Adrian Tinniswood, *By Permission of Heaven: The Story of the Great Fire of London* (New York: Riverhead Books, 2004), pp. 20–24.

2. Neil Hanson, *The Great Fire of London: In That Apocalyptic Year, 1666* (New York: John Wiley, 2002), p. 49.

3. John Evelyn, *Diary and Correspondence of John Evelyn, F.R.S.* (London: Hurst and Blackett, 1854), p. 11.

4. Hanson, pp. 134–138.

5. Ibid., pp. 244–246.

6. Ibid., p. 235.

7. Evelyn, p. 10.

Chapter 2. The Rise and Fall of Rome

1. Michael Crawford, *The Roman Republic, Second Edition* (Cambridge, MA: Harvard University Press, 2006), pp. 31–42.

2. Kate Gilliver, *Caesar's Gallic Wars, 58–50 B.C.* (New York: Routledge, 2003), pp. 69–79.

3. Antony Kamm, *Julius Caesar: A Life* (New York: Routledge, 2006), pp. 139–148.

4. Ramon L. Jimenez, *Caesar Against Rome: The Great Roman Civil War* (Westport, CT: Praeger, 2000), pp. 248–249.

5. Ibid., pp. 1–6.

6. Pat Southern, *The Roman Empire from Severus to Constantine* (New York: Routledge, 2001), pp. 169–181.

7. Stephen Mitchell, *A History of the Later Roman Empire, AD 284–641: The Transformation of the Ancient World* (Malden, MA: Blackwell Publishing Co., 2006), p. 101.

8. Prudence Jones, *Cleopatra: A Sourcebook* (Norman: University of Oklahoma Press, 2006), pp. 3–30.

9. Plutarch on Antony and Cleopatra, the Last of the Ptolemies, http://www.shsu.edu/~his_ncp/AntCleo.html

10. Jones, pp. 94–128.

Chapter 3. The Middle Ages

1. Pierre Riche, *The Carolingians: A Family Who Forged Europe*, translated by Michael Idomir Allen (Philadelphia: University of Pennsylvania Press, 1993), pp. 130–131.

2. Ibid., pp. 94–95.

3. Medieval Sourcebook: Crisis, Recovery, Feudalism? http://www.fordham.edu/halsall/sbook1i.html#Feudalism

4. Riche, p. 43.

5. David Howarth, *1066: The Year of the Conquest* (New York: Barnes and Noble, 1993), pp. 166–184.

6. British Library Treasures in Full: Magna Carta, http://www.bl.uk/treasures/magnacarta/magna.html

7. William C. Jordan, *The Great Famine: Northern Europe in the Early Fourteenth Century* (Princeton, NJ: University of Princeton Press, 1996), pp. 3–5.

8. Barbara Rosenwein, *A Short History of the Middle Ages* (Orchard Park, NY: Broadview Press, 2004), p. 169.

9. R.L. Storey and Neville Williams, editors, *Chronology of the Medieval World: 800 to 1491* (New York: D. McKay Co., 1973), pp. 600–625.

10. Plague, http://www.brown.edu/
Departments/Italian_Studies/dweb/
plague/perspectives/de_mussi.shtml

Chapter 4. The Golden Age
1. Jerry Brotton, *The Renaissance*
(New York: Oxford University Press,
2006), pp. 22–28.
2. Ibid., p. 63.
3. Roger J. Crum and John T.
Paoletti, editors, *Renaissance Florence:
A Social History* (New York: Cambridge
University Press, 2006), pp. 267–270.
4. Images of Renaissance Art:
Italian Painting, http://history.hanover.
edu/courses/art/111ren.html
5. Thomas F. Arnold, *The
Renaissance at War* (Washington, DC:
Smithsonian History of Warfare, 2006),
pp. 140–146.
6. Leonardo da Vinci: Renaissance
Man, http://www.mos.org/leonardo/bio.
html
7. Henry Kamen, *The Spanish
Inquisition: A Historical Revision* (New
Haven: Yale University Press, 1998),
pp. 75–78.
8. Friedrich von Schiller, *Revolt of
Netherlands* (Whitefish, MT: Kessinger
Publishing, 2004), pp. 52–57.
9. Peter H. Wilson, *The Holy
Roman Empire, 1495–1806* (New York:
St. Martin's Press, 1999), p. 18.
10. Holy Roman Empire,
http://encarta.msn.com/encyclopedia_
761558731/Holy_Roman_Empire.html
11. Wilson, p. 82.

Chapter 5. The Old Regime Turns New
1. John Henry, *The Scientific
Revolution and the Origins of Modern
Science* (New York: Palgrave
Macmillan, 2002), pp. 96–97.
2. Emmanuel Le Roy Ladurie, *The
Ancien Regime: A History of France,
1610–1774*, translated by Mark
Greengrass (Cambridge: Blackwell
Publishers, 1996), pp. 1–25.
3. Ibid., p. 95.
4. Donald M. Kagan, Steven
Ozment, and Frank M. Turner, *The
Western Heritage, Combined, Eighth
Edition* (New York: Prentice Hall,
2004), pp. 235–236.
5. Frank McLynn, *1759: The Year
Britain Became Master of the World*
(London: Jonathan Cape, 2004),
pp. 22–53.
6. Ibid., pp. 388–392.
7. Dena Goodman, *The Republic
of Letters: A Cultural History of the
French Enlightenment* (New York:
Cornell University Press, 1996),
pp. 1–10.
8. John Henry, *The Scientific
Revolution and the Origins of Modern
Science* (New York: Palgrave
Macmillan, 2002), pp. 15–21.
9. Ibid., p. 18.
10. Ibid., pp. 110–111.

Chapter 6. A Time of Revolution
1. Dena Goodman, *The Republic
of Letters: A Cultural History of the
French Enlightenment* (New York:
Cornell University Press, 1996),
pp. 1–10.
2. Jack R. Censer and Lynn Avery
Hunt, *Liberty, Equality, Fraternity:
Exploring the French Revolution*
(Philadelphia: Pennsylvania State
University Press, 2001), p. 86.

3. David Andress, *The Terror: The Merciless War for Freedom in Revolutionary France* (New York: Farrar, Straus, and Giroux, 2006), pp. 1–8.

4. Ibid., pp. 145–146.

5. Ibid., pp. 289–290.

6. Napoleon.org, http://www.napoleon.org

7. Owen Connelly, *Wars of the French Revolution and Napoleonic Era* (New York: Routledge, 2005), pp. 123–124.

8. Ibid., pp. 58–62, 75–76.

9. Ibid., pp. 198–199.

10. Ibid., p. 214.

11. Captain Rees Howell Gronow, *Captain Gronow's Last Recollections*, London: Smith, Elder, and Company, 1866; *Napoleonic Literature*, Book 32, Section 7, http://napoleonic-literature.com/Book_32/Section007.htm

12. Andress, p. 12.

13. Marie Antoinette, Louis XVI and the French Revolution, http://www.royalty.nu/Europe/France/MarieAntoinette.html

14. Marie Antoinette and the French Revolution, http://www.pbs.org/marieantoinette/index.html

Chapter 7. A Century of Isms

1. The Congress of Vienna, http://www2.sunysuffolk.edu/westn/congvienna.html

2. Alan S. Kahan, *Liberalism in Nineteenth-Century Europe: The Political Culture of Limited Suffrage* (New York: Palgrave Macmillan, 2003), pp. 1–10.

3. John Hutchinson, *Nationalism* (New York: Oxford University Press, 1995), pp. 36–45.

4. Kahan, pp. 66–141.

5. Ibid., pp. 21–30.

6. Louis XVIII, http://gallery.sjsu.edu/paris/politics/LouisXVIII00.htm

7. Donald M. Kagan, Steven Ozment, and Frank M. Turner, *The Western Heritage, Combined, Eighth Edition* (New York: Prentice Hall, 2004), pp. 333–334.

8. Louis XVIII, http://gallery.sjsu.edu/paris/politics/LouisXVIII00.htm

9. Charles X, http://gallery.sjsu.edu/paris/politics/Charles00.htm

10. Louis Philippe, http://gallery.sjsu.edu/paris/politics/Louisphilippe00.htm

11. The Great Reform Act, http://www.learningcurve.gov.uk/politics/g6/

12. Kagan, p. 532.

Chapter 8. The Birth of the Nation-State

1. E.J. Hobsbawn with Chris Wrigley, *Industry and Empire: The Birth of the Industrial Revolution* (New York: New Press, 1999), pp. 87–111.

2. James Matthew Thompson, *Louis Napoleon and the Second Empire* (New York: Columbia University Press, 1984), pp. 1–12.

3. Crimean War Research Society, http://www.crimeanwar.org/cwrsentry.html

4. James Matthew Thompson, *Louis Napoleon and the Second Empire* (New York: Columbia University Press, 1984), pp. 176–178.

5. David G. Williamson, *Germany Since 1815: A Nation Forged and Renewed* (New York: Palgrave Macmillan, 2005), pp. 17–27, 30–32.

6. Ibid., p. 81.

7. Ibid., p. 115.

8. Hobsbawn, pp. 112–131.

9. Liverpool and Manchester, http://www.spartacus.schoolnet.co.uk/RAliverpool.htm

10. Joseph A. Montagna, "The Industrial Revolution." http://www.yale.edu/ynhti/curriculum/units/1981/2/81.02.06.x.html

Chapter 9. Imperialism and the Great War

1. Philip D. Curtin, *The World and the West: The European Challenge and the Overseas Response in the Age of Empire* (Cambridge: Cambridge University Press, 2002), pp. 3–18.

2. Ibid., pp. 28–32.

3. Ibid., pp. 36–41.

4. Modern History Sourcebook: A War Correspondent in the Franco-Prussian War, 1870, http://www.fordham.edu/halsall/mod/1870war1.html. The Franco-Prussian War was one of the first of the nineteenth-century wars to have war correspondents. The Crimean War in the 1850s was on the cutting edge of this trend.

5. Ibid.

6. David G. Williamson, *Germany Since 1815: A Nation Forged and Renewed* (New York: Palgrave Macmillan, 2005), pp. 112–117, 129.

7. Ibid., p. 131.

8. Martin Gilbert, *The First World War: A Complete History* (New York: Henry Holt, 1994), pp. 1–15.

9. Ibid., pp. 517–522.

10. John Ellis, *Eye-deep in Hell: Trench Warfare in World War I* (Baltimore: Johns Hopkins University Press, 1989), p. 24.

11. First World War.com, http://www.firstworldwar.com/atoz/bigbertha.htm

12. Ellis, pp. 65–68.

Chapter 10. World War II and the Cold War

1. James L. Stokesbury, *A Short History of World War II* (New York: Harper Paperbacks, 1980), pp. 39–41.

2. Ibid., pp. 177–179.

3. Ibid., pp. 150–160.

4. John Lewis Gaddis, *The Cold War: A New History* (New York: Penguin, 2006), pp. 28–32.

5. Ibid., pp. 30–36.

6. Ibid., pp. 34–39.

7. Ibid., pp. 233–240.

8. Holocaust Encyclopedia, http://www.ushmm.org/wlc/en/index.php?lang=en&ModuleId=10005143

Chapter 11. From Iron Curtain to European Union

1. John Lewis Gaddis, *The Cold War: A New History* (New York: Penguin, 2006), p. 95.

2. Ibid., pp. 121–132.

3. Simon Hix, *The Political System of the European Union* (New York: Palgrave Macmillan, 2005), pp. 3, 26, 173.

4. Ibid., p. 26.

5. Ibid., p. 112.

6. Ibid., p. 27.

7. Tommaso Padoa-Schioppa, *The Euro and Its Central Bank: Getting United After the Union* (Cambridge: The MIT Press, 2004), pp. 1–20.

8. David G. Williamson, *Germany Since 1815: A Nation Forged and Renewed* (New York: Palgrave Macmillan, 2005), pp. 288–301.

9. Ibid., pp. 301, 333, 367.

Books

Ackroyd, Peter. *Ancient Rome*. New York: Dorling Kindersley, 2005.

Barter, James. *The Late Middle Ages*. Detroit: Lucent Books, 2006.

Bingham, Marjorie Wall. *An Age of Empires, 1200–1750*. New York: Oxford University Press, 2005.

Burgan, Michael. *Empire of Ancient Rome*. New York: Facts On File, 2005.

Fitzgerald, Brian. *Under Fire in World War II*. Chicago: Raintree, 2006.

Goldstein, Margaret J. *World War II: Europe*. Minneapolis: Lerner Publications, 2004.

Grant, R.G. *World War I*. Farmington Hills, MI: Lucent Books, 2005.

Greenblatt, Miriam. *Napoleon Bonaparte and Imperial France*. New York: Marshall Cavendish Benchmark, 2006.

Hanawalt, Barbara. *The European World, 400–1450*. New York: Oxford University Press, 2005.

Murrell, Deborah Jane. *The Best Book of Ancient Rome*. Boston: Kingfisher, 2004.

Schomp, Virginia. *The Italian Renaissance*. New York: Benchmark Books, 2003.

Sirimarco, Elizabeth. *The Cold War*. New York: Benchmark Books, 2005.

Works Consulted

Andress, David. *The Terror: The Merciless War for Freedom in Revolutionary France*. New York: Farrar, Straus, and Giroux, 2006.

Arnold, Thomas F. *The Renaissance at War*. Washington, D.C.: Smithsonian History of Warfare, 2006.

Brotton, Jerry. *The Renaissance*. New York: Oxford University Press, 2006.

Censer, Jack R., and Lynn Avery Hunt. *Liberty, Equality, Fraternity: Exploring the French Revolution*. Philadelphia: Pennsylvania State University Press, 2001.

Connelly, Owen. *Wars of the French Revolution and Napoleonic Era*. New York: Routledge, 2005.

Crawford, Michael. *The Roman Republic, Second Edition*. Cambridge, Massachusetts: Harvard University Press, 2006.

Crum, Roger J., and John T. Paoletti, editors. *Renaissance Florence: A Social History*. New York: Cambridge University Press, 2006.

Curtin, Philip D. *The World and the West: The European Challenge and the Overseas Response in the Age of Empire*. New York: Cambridge University Press, 2002.

Ellis, John. *Eye-deep in Hell: Trench Warfare in World War I*. Baltimore: Johns Hopkins University Press, 1989.

Evelyn, John. *Diary and Correspondence of John Evelyn, F.R.S*. London: Hurst and Blackett, 1854.

Gaddis, John Lewis. *The Cold War: A New History*. New York: Penguin, 2006.

Gilbert, Martin. *The First World War: A Complete History*. New York: Henry Holt, 1994.

Gilliver, Kate. *Caesar's Gallic Wars, 58–50 B.C.* New York: Routledge, 2003.

Goodman, Dena. *The Republic of Letters: A Cultural History of the French Enlightenment*. New York: Cornell University Press, 1996.

Hanson, Neil. *The Great Fire of London: In That Apocalyptic Year, 1666*. New York: John Wiley, 2002.

Henry, John. *The Scientific Revolution and the Origins of Modern Science.* New York: Palgrave Macmillan, 2002.

Hix, Simon. *The Political System of the European Union.* New York: Palgrave Macmillan, 2005.

Hobsbawn, E.J., and Chris Wrigley. *Industry and Empire: The Birth of the Industrial Revolution.* New York: New Press, 1999.

Howarth, David. *1066: The Year of the Conquest.* New York: Barnes and Noble, 1993.

Hutchinson, John. *Nationalism.* New York: Oxford University Press, 1995.

Jimenez, Ramon L. *Caesar Against Rome: The Great Roman Civil War.* Westport, CT: Praeger, 2000.

Jones, Prudence. *Cleopatra: A Sourcebook.* Norman, Oklahoma: University of Oklahoma Press, 2006.

Jordan, William C. *The Great Famine: Northern Europe in the Early Fourteenth Century.* Princeton, NJ: University of Princeton Press, 1996.

Kagan, Donald M., Steven Ozment and Frank M. Turner. *The Western Heritage, Combined, Eighth Edition.* New York: Prentice Hall, 2004.

Kahan, Alan S. *Liberalism in Nineteenth-Century Europe: The Political Culture of Limited Suffrage.* New York: Palgrave Macmillan, 2003.

Kamen, Henry. *The Spanish Inquisition: A Historical Revision.* New Haven, Connecticut: Yale University Press, 1998.

Kamm, Antony. *Julius Caesar: A Life.* New York: Routledge, 2006.

Ladurie, Emmanuel Le Roy. *The Ancien Regime: A History of France, 1610–1774.* Translated by Mark Greengrass. Cambridge: Blackwell Publishers, 1996.

McLynn, Frank. *1759: The Year Britain Became Master of the World.* London: Jonathan Cape, 2004.

Mitchell, Stephen. *A History of the Later Roman Empire, AD 284-641: The Transformation of the Ancient World.* Malden, MA: Blackwell Publishing Co., 2006.

Padoa-Schioppa, Tommaso. *The Euro and Its Central Bank: Getting United After the Union.* Cambridge: The MIT Press, 2004.

Pounds, Norman. *An Historical Geography of Europe, 1500–1840.* Cambridge: Cambridge University Press, 1979.

———. *An Historical Geography of Europe, 1800–1914.* Cambridge: Cambridge University Press, 1985.

Riche, Pierre. *The Carolingians: A Family Who Forged Europe.* Translated by Michael Idomir Allen Philadelphia: University of Pennsylvania Press, 1993.

Rosenwein, Barbara. *A Short History of the Middle Ages.* Orchard Park, NY: Broadview Press, 2004.

Southern, Pat. *The Roman Empire from Severus to Constantine.* New York: Routledge, 2001.

Stokesbury, James L. *A Short History of World War II.* New York: Harper Paperbacks, 1980.

Storey, R.L., and Neville Williams, ed. *Chronology of the Medieval World: 800 to 1491.* New York: D. McKay Co., 1973.

Further Reading

Thompson, James Matthew. *Louis Napoleon and the Second Empire*. New York: Columbia University Press, 1984.

Time-Life Books. *What Life Was Like When Rome Ruled the World: The Roman Empire, 100 BC–AD 200*. Alexandria, VA: Time-Life Books, 1997.

Tinniswood, Adrian. *By Permission of Heaven: The Story of the Great Fire of London*. New York: Riverhead Books, 2004.

von Schiller, Friedrich. *Revolt of Netherlands*. Whitefish, MT: Kessinger Publishing, 2004.

Williamson, David G. *Germany Since 1815: A Nation Forged and Renewed*. New York: Palgrave Macmillan, 2005.

Wilson, Peter H. *The Holy Roman Empire, 1495–1806*. New York: St. Martin's Press, 1999.

On the Internet

Charles X http://gallery.sjsu.edu/paris/politics/Charles00.htm

The Cold War Museum http://www.coldwar.org/index.html

Crimean War Research Society http://www.crimeanwar.org/cwrsentry.html

First World War.com http://www.firstworldwar.com/atoz/bigbertha.htm

Friedrich Ludwig Jahn, Father of Gymnastics http://www.gymmedia.com/jahn/E_index.htm

History of Europe: The Periodical Historical Atlas, 1100 to 2000 http://www.euratlas.com/time2.htm

Holocaust Encyclopedia http://www.ushmm.org/wlc/en/index.php?lang=en&ModuleId=10005143

Joseph A. Montagna, "The Industrial Revolution." http://www.yale.edu/ynhti/curriculum/units/1981/2/81.02.06.x.html

Liberty, Equality, Fraternity: Exploring the French Revolution http://chnm.gmu.edu/revolution/

Louis Philippe http://gallery.sjsu.edu/paris/politics/Louisphilippe00.htm

Louis XVIII http://gallery.sjsu.edu/paris/politics/LouisXVIII00.htm

Marie Antoinette and the French Revolution http://www.pbs.org/marieantoinette/index.html

Medieval Europe http://www.mnsu.edu/emuseum/history/middleages/

Modern History Sourcebook: A War Correspondent in the Franco-Prussian War, 1870 http://www.fordham.edu/halsall/mod/1870war1.html

Museum of World War II http://museumofworldwarii.com/Tour.htm

Napoleon.org http://www.napoleon.org

Napoleonic Literature http://www.napoleonic-literature.com/index.html

Plague http://www.brown.edu/Departments/Italian_Studies/dweb/plague/perspectives/de_mussi.shtml

Plutarch on Antony and Cleopatra, the Last of the Ptolemies http://www.shsu.edu/~his_ncp/AntCleo.html

Renaissance http://www.learner.org/exhibits/renaissance/

The Roman Empire in the First Century http://www.pbs.org/empires/romans/index.html

anarchy (AA-nar-kee)—The absence of government or system of laws.

armistice (AR-muh-stuss)—An agreement to stop fighting.

bureaucracies (byoo-RAH-kruh-seez)—Government administrations with many officials and rules.

chivalry (SHIH-vul-ree)—A system of beliefs among knights in the Middle Ages that emphasized honor, generosity, courtesy, and bravery.

communism (KAH-myoo-nism)—A system of government in which the state owns all property and the means of producing and distributing goods, in theory so that everything can be shared in common.

coup (KOO)—A sudden overthrow of a government.

demographic (deh-moh-GRAH-fik)—Referring to the traits that make up a population or group of people.

entrepreneurs (on-truh-preh-NOORS)—People who are willing to take risks in starting up a business.

exodus (EK-suh-dus)—A mass migration out of a certain area.

Hapsburg Empire—Beginning in 1526, lands occupied largely by Germanic peoples under the rule of the House of Hapsburg. The Hapsburg Empire officially became the Austrian Empire in 1804, and then became Austria-Hungary in 1867. The Austrian-Hungary Empire disbanded at the end of World War I.

humanism (HYOO-muh-nism)—A philosophy developed during the Renaissance urging all people to seek truth in their own characters and not just in religious teachings.

imperialism (im-PEER-ee-ul-ism)—The government, authority, or system of an empire.

inflation (in-FLAY-shun)—A steady increase in prices.

Iron Curtain—The symbolic division between Eastern and Western Europe lasting from the end of World War II to the end of the Cold War; the phrase originated with British Prime Minister Winston Churchill.

orator (OR-uh-tor)—A person who is very good at public speaking.

papacy (PAY-puh-see)—Referring to the office of the Pope of the Catholic Church.

patrons (PAY-truns)—People who provide support, usually financial, to artists.

Punic Wars (PYOO-nik wars)—A series of three wars between the Roman Republic and Carthage, a city in North Africa, that began when the Romans tried to expand into Carthaginian territory. The first Punic War ran from 264 to 241 BCE, the second from 218 to 202 BCE, and the third from 149 to 146 BCE, when Carthage was destroyed.

republicanism (ree-PUB-lih-kun-ism)—An idea dating back to ancient Rome stressing that a country's people, and not the monarchy, should be the ruling body. According to this idea, the government should exist merely to protect the liberty and equality of its citizens, and not to rule them arbitrarily or tax them heavily.

sacked—Captured (a city) and then plundered it by stripping it of its valuables.

scaffolding (SKAA-ful-ding)—A temporary framework, frequently made of wood, that allows people to work above ground level to construct or repair a building.

Spanish Inquisition (in-kwih-ZIH-shun)—The attempt by King Ferdinand and Queen Isabella to make Catholicism the official (and only) religion of Spain. Starting in 1478, tribunals tried many non-Catholics of heresy; many of those tried were tortured and executed.

status quo (STAA-tus KWOH)—The existing way of doing things.

Visigoths (VIH-sih-goths)—Germanic peoples who helped bring about the downfall of the Western Roman Empire.

Index

Actium, Battle of   20, 21, 23
Africa   16, 17, 18, 20, 37, 73, 89
Aix-la-Chapelle, Treaty of   43
Alfonso I   35
Anjou   27
Antony, Mark   20, 23
Aquitaine   27
Aristotle   47
Articles of the Barons   28
Asia   73
Augustus, Romulus   22
Augustus Caesar   19, 21, 22
Austria   42, 44, 47, 52, 53, 55, 57–59, 65–69, 71, 74–78, 81, 91
Austria-Hungary   75
Austro-Prussian War   69

Bacon, Sir Francis   47
Barbados   41
Barroso, Jose Manuel   94
Bastille   49, 50
Belgium   61, 75, 78, 90
Benelux   91
Berlin Wall   95
Bermuda   41
Big Bertha   79
Bismarck, Otto von   68–69, 74, 75
Black Death   29, 31, 33
Bloodworth, Sir Thomas   9
Bonaparte, Napoleon   39, 48, 51–54, 58, 63
Bonaparte, Louis-Napoleon (Napoleon III)   65, 66, 70
Bosnia   75
Botticelli   34, 35
Bulgaria   94

Caesar, Julius   18–20, 23
Caribbean Sea   40, 41
Carlsbad Decrees   60
Carthage   17, 18

Charlemagne (Charles the Great)   25, 26, 27, 28, 34, 36, 39, 47
Charles II   10, 11, 12, 13, 15
Charles X, King of France   60, 61, 71
Charles V, King of Spain   32, 37, 38, 47
Charles VIII, King of France   35
Charles Martel   25, 26
China   73
Christianity   25, 33–34
Churchill, Winston   82, 84
Cleopatra   19, 20, 23
Cold War   81, 83–86, 88, 89
Commodus   22
Communist Party   84
Confederation of the Rhine   52, 53
Constantine, Emporer   21, 22, 23
Constantinople   21, 22, 33, 34, 36
Constitutional monarchy   50, 59, 61
Containment   84
Convention of Westminster   62
Copernicus, Nicolaus   47
Crassus, Marcus   18, 19
Crimean War   67–69
Czechoslovakia   78, 8, 89
Czech Republic   69

Denmark   78, 93, 94
Descartes, Rene   47
Diocletian   22
Dual Alliance   74
Duchy of Warsaw   52, 53

Edward II, King of England   29
Egypt   19, 21, 23, 90
Eleanor of Aquitaine   27
Elba   53, 54
Enlightenment   43, 44, 45, 49, 57
Entente Cordiale   75, 76
Estonia   78
Etruscans   17

Index

Euro   93, 94
European Coal and Steel Community
   90
European Economic Community (EEC)
   90–94, 95
European Free Trade Area (EFTA)   88,
   91
European Union (EU)   86, 88, 90–91,
   92, 93–94
Evelyn, John   11, 12, 15

Farriner, Thomas   9, 14, 19
Feudal system   25, 27, 29, 50
Finland   78
First Triumvirate   18, 19, 20
Five Good Emperors   22
Florence   34, 35
Fontenoy, Battle of   43
France   27, 29, 30, 31, 33, 35, 40,
   41–46, 49–54, 55, 57, 58, 59, 60,
   65–69, 74–78, 81–83, 89, 90, 91,
   93, 95
Francia   25
Franco-Prussian War   70, 74
Franco-Russian Alliance   75, 76
Frankfurt Parliament   67
Franks   25, 27
Franz Ferdinand, Archduke of Austria-
   Hungary   75
Frederick II (the Great), King of
   Prussia   42, 43, 44, 46
Frederick William III, King of Prussia
   52, 60
French and Indian War   43–44
French Revolution (1789)   49–52, 54,
   55
French Revolution (1830)   61, 65

Gallic Wars   18–19
Gascony   27

Gaul   18, 19, 21, 25
Genoa   31, 33
German Confederation   59, 68
Germany   31, 33, 37, 38, 39, 42, 52,
   53, 58, 65–70, 71, 74–78, 80,
   81–84, 87, 89–91, 93, 95
Great Britain   41, 43–44, 57, 58, 62,
   67, 68, 71, 73–76, 77, 78, 82,
   89–91, 93, 94, 95
Great Depression   81
Great Famine   29
Great Fire of London   8, 9–15
Gymnastics   63

Hapsburg Empire   42
Hastings, Battle of   26, 27, 28
Henry II, King of England   27
Herculaneum   22
High Middle Ages   26, 28
Hitler, Adolf   80, 81, 82, 87
Holocaust   81, 87
Holstein   68
Holy Roman Empire   39, 52
House of Commons, Great Britain
   62
Hubert, Robert   15
Hume, David   45, 46
Hundred Years' War   24, 27, 29, 30
Hungary   66, 75, 77

Industrial Revolution   62, 65, 66, 68,
   71
Ireland   27, 93
Iron Curtain   89, 91, 93
Isabella II, Queen of Spain   69, 70
Islam   25
Israel   87
Italy   17, 25, 33, 35, 36, 37, 53, 58,
   65–66, 68, 75, 76, 82, 83, 90
Italian Wars   35–36

Index

Jamaica 41
James, Duke of York 12
Japan 82–83
Joan of Arc 29, 30
John I, King of England 28
John XII, Pope 39

Königgrätz, Battle of 69
Kossuth, Louis 65–66
Kunersdorff, Battle of 45

Latvia 78
Leo III, Pope 25
Leonardo da Vinci 35, 36
Leopold 69
Lepidus 20
Lithuania 78
Liverpool and Manchester Railway
    71
Louis VIII 59
Louis XVI, King of France 49, 50, 51,
    55
Louis-Philippe, King of France 60,
    61, 65
Luther, Martin 37
Luxembourg 90, 91

Maastricht, Treaty of 93–94
Machiavelli 34
Magna Carta 28
Marcus Junius Brutus 20
Maria Theresa, Empress of the
    Hapsburg Empire 42, 44
Marie Antoinette 49, 50, 55
Marshall Plan 85, 90
Medici family 34, 35
Metternich, Klemens von 58, 59, 60,
    66
Michelangelo 34, 36
Middle Ages 26–30, 31, 33

Middle East 20
Milan 35
Montesquieu, Baron de 45
Mount Vesuvius 22
Mussolini, Benito 82, 83

Naples 32, 35
Napoleon III (see Bonaparte,
    Louis-Napoleon)
Napoleonic Empire 48
Napoleonic Wars 49, 56
National Socialist German Worker's
    Party (Nazi Party) 81, 83, 87
Nero 22
Nerva 22
Netherlands 37, 38, 61, 90
Newton, Sir Isaac 47
Nicholas V, Pope 35
Normandy 27
Normans 26, 27
North America 40, 41–42, 44
North Atlantic Treaty Organization
    (NATO) 85, 90, 95
Norway 91, 93

Octavian 20, 21, 23
Odoacer 22
Old Regime 41–46
Ostrogoths 25
Otto I, Holy Roman Emperor 39
Ottoman Empire 68

Pearl Harbor 82–83, 85
Philip II, King of Spain 38
Piedmont 66, 68
Pisa 33
Plutarch 23
Poland 78, 82, 89
Pompeii 22
Pompey the Great 18, 19, 23

Index

Portugal   25, 31, 91
Protestant Reformation   37
Prussia   42, 43, 57, 58, 64
Ptolemy XIII   19, 23
Punic Wars   17, 18

Reign of Terror   51
Renaissance   33–38, 41
Rhineland   81
Robespierre, Maximilien   51
Romans   17, 21, 33
Rome, Treaty of   90, 91
Roman Empire   16, 21, 22, 23, 23
Roman Empire, Eastern   22, 33
Roman Empire, Western   22, 25, 33
Romania   94
Roman Republic   17, 21, 66
Roosevelt, Franklin D.   84
Rousseau, Jean-Jacques   45, 46
Russia   31, 37, 68, 74–75, 76, 77,
    78, 82
Russian Revolution   76

Saxons   25
Schleswig   68
Second Triumvirate   20
Serbia   75
Seven Years' War   40, 41–45, 49
Sforza, Francesco   35
Silesia   42, 43
Soviet Union   80, 82–86, 90, 95
Spain   25, 31, 35–38, 69, 70
Spanish Inquisition   38
Stalin, Joseph   84
Sudetenland   81
Suez Canal   90
Sweden   52, 91, 93
Switzerland   61, 91

Theodosius I   22
Touraine   27
Tours, Battle of   25, 26, 28
Trafalgar, Battle of   52, 53, 67
Trajan   22
Trench warfare   79
Triple Alliance   75, 77
Triple Entente   75, 76

United States   78, 82–86, 87, 90, 93
University of Paris   26
U.S.S.R.   (see Soviet Union)

Venice   31, 33, 34, 35
Vercingetorix   19
Versailles, Treaty of   78, 81
Vesalius, Andreas   47
Vienna   52, 57, 58, 61, 66
Visigoths   21, 22, 25
Voltaire, François-Marie Arouet de
    39, 47

War of Austrian Succession   42, 43
War of Jenkins' Ear   42
Warsaw Pact   85
Waterloo, Battle of   53, 54
West Indies   40, 42
Whitehall Palace   12
William I, King of Prussia   69
William II, of Germany   75
William the Conqueror, the Duke of
    Normandy   27
William, Prince of Orange   38
World War I   70, 72, 75–78, 79, 81
World War II   80, 81–83, 87

Yalta Conference   84
Yugoslavia   77, 78

About the Author

Frances E. Davey is a historian working on her PhD in American History at the University of Delaware. She also finds European History fascinating, particularly because so much of American History is European in origin. When she does research, Davey examines both primary documents—documents that people wrote in the past—and material culture. Material culture, the study of society through objects, can tell us a lot about how people lived long ago.

Before becoming an academic, Davey worked in several small museums around the country. She has been an educator at the Peabody Essex Museum in Salem, Massachusetts; a collections manager at the Treasure Island Museum in San Francisco, California; and the curator of collections at Burritt Museum and Park in Huntsville, Alabama. She loves traveling and meeting people from different places. In her spare time, she enjoys distance running, quilting, and playing with her nephew.